# BACKPACK

## On the Trail of Vlad "the Impaler" Dracula and the Vampire He Inspired

## By Leif Pettersen

facebook.com/BackpackingwithDracula

## @ImpalerEnabler

Bleh.

# Chapters

# Acknowledgements

Usually these Acknowledgements sections can go on for pages, thanking the small army of people involved in getting a print book published. Well, this is a self-published book, so I didn't have that kind of support. It should thus be noted the people mentioned here were *especially* crucial to getting this book out for lack of the usual resources.

Liz Puhl not only spent copious time getting the 15th-century maps in this book looking as accurate as possible, but she also proofread all manner of material, including the book proposal and sample chapters, as well as helped with cover art mock-ups.

Gina Czupka and Doug Mack agreed to read a lengthy, early draft of the full manuscript and, thankfully, they largely agreed on what needed to be changed to make the content flow better.

Brendan Kennealy was a late, though substantial contributor, swooping in and providing some critical copy editing and humor feedback on the newly engorged manuscript, which he somehow completed outside of his full-time job in a blistering nine days.

A number of friends and fellow writers kindly referred me to literary agents, all 35 of whom rejected my book proposal, so obviously screw those guys.

Kudos and thanks go to the *Backpacking with Dracula* Facebook group for support, cover feedback, promotional assistance and the alternative titles *Dracpacking* and *Backpackula*.

Finally, there were innumerable people who generously provided critical nuggets of encouragement, guidance, and introductions along the way, some of which I ignored, but all of it was appreciated nonetheless. Thank you.

## Eastern Europe and Asia Minor, circa mid-15th century

Sources: Natural Earth (naturalearthdata.com); *Historical Atlas* by
William Shepherd (New York: Henry Holt and Company, 1911).

# Wallachia, Transylvania, and Moldavia, mid-15th century

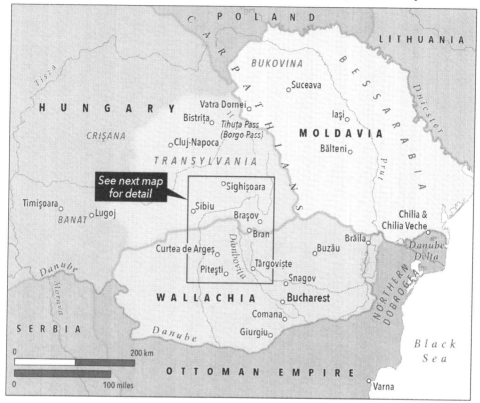

Sources: Natural Earth (naturalearthdata.com); *Historical Atlas* by
William Shepherd (New York: Henry Holt and Company, 1911);
Wikipedia article "Transylvania."

# Southern Transylvania and Northern Wallachia (Vlad's stomping grounds)

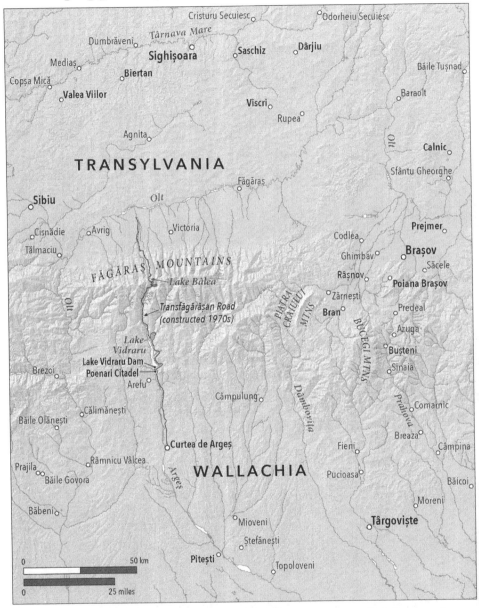

Sources: OpenStreetMap (openstreetmap.org); Jarvis A., H.I. Reuter, A. Nelson, E. Guevara, 2008, Hole-filled seamless SRTM data V4, International Centre for Tropical Agriculture (CIAT), available from srtm.csi.cgiar.org.

# Introduction

From the dirt parking lot by the road, you have to climb 1,480 steps to reach Vlad "The Impaler" Dracula's home/stronghold/babe lair, Poenari Citadel[1], located in the mountains of northern Wallachia near the border with Transylvania. It was March 2006, the tail end of a particularly brutal winter in Romania and, due to deadlines set by some editor in balmy Melbourne, I was forced to undertake my very first Romania guidebook research trip for Lonely Planet while heavy snow and ice remained on roads that weren't particularly safe even in perfect weather.

It was also still cold enough to freeze to death in one's car should it break down miles from anywhere, as I was at the time. For reasons that I swear made perfect sense in the moment, the car in which I had entrusted my dumb safety was a 1990 Dacia 1310, a choice that ultimately wilted into regret akin to a Mitt Romney face tattoo. From the day they rolled off the assembly line, these old Dacias were never in perfect working order—they were just momentarily not broken.

I'd already shaken the muffler partly loose, which, in the proud Romanian tradition of quick and dirty Dacia repairs, I had re-secured to the car's undercarriage with twine I found in my trunk. Days later, after I drove the car through a snow-obscured pothole big enough to hide

---

[1] A.k.a. Poenari Castle.

another car, the muffler fell off completely, joining the countless other Dacia mufflers littering Romania's motorways like roadkill.

The crazy research pace I was keeping, the near constant stress over my car breaking down every other day, the relentless white-knuckle driving conditions and the godforsaken, unremitting chill had all combined to break down my immune system and saddle me with a nasty cold. And I wasn't even halfway through the trip.

Yet there I was, utterly alone, trudging up a snowy mountainside to investigate the ruined, possibly demon-infested home of one of history's cruelest and most violent individuals in a country where even now you can find people who are *certain* that vampires are real.

And then it hit me: this is exactly how idiots die in horror movies. You know what I mean. Some soon-to-be-screaming dumbass sets off alone to investigate something freaky, then makes a series of decisions escalating in stupidity. If it's a woman, she'll be holding a weak, dying flashlight and wearing nothing but a nightgown the consistency of discount Kleenex; if it's a guy, he'll stop for a snack or a pee, realizing only when it's too late that his shotgun is well out of reach. Whatever the case, the audience senses the machete-bait's disembowelment a full five minutes before it happens.

Absent shotgun and nightgown notwithstanding, my predicament was cinematically perfect.

Yes, even more than five centuries after his death, Dracula can still give otherwise self-possessed people the creeps. And that was before I learned all the alarming things I know about him today.

--------------------------------------

"Why did I write this book?" That's what I'm supposed to explain here, if I am to trust travel book structure guidelines I downloaded for free off the internet. I guess the root answer is because I thought it needed to be done; untangling and illustrating the fact, legend and myth of one of the most famous, nightmare-summoning names in popular culture, all while exploring his home turf.

Both Prince Vlad III Dracula and Count Dracula—hereafter I shall use "Draculae" as the plural of Dracula—are among the most intriguing characters in history and fiction, not to mention all the blurry wrinkles in between[2]. Unfortunately, both of them suffered from likeability deficiencies, particularly in regard to their legacies and subsequent confusion of their identities.

Vlad Dracula was the victim of a hog-pile, post-mortem smear campaign that makes Romanian ex-dictator Nicolae Ceaușescu's legacy seem as wholesome as Santa Claus's. Vlad's name then faded into murky legend at best and complete obscurity at worst, except in Romania where

---

[2] Vlad, despite being a real guy, was most certainly a character, as we will quickly learn.

he's still considered a heroic combination of Robin Hood and Rambo.

Ironically, Vlad's namesake in Bram Stoker's 1897 novel *Dracula*, an actual murderous, blood-swilling monster mind you, is downright gentlemanly and low-key by comparison. And, double-ironically, he was probably responsible for far fewer deaths over the course of his existence than ol' Vlad. Over time, as the fictional Dracula character was recycled in various forms of media, writers warped and embellished his personality, hunger and powers to instill ever greater fright in their increasingly blasé audiences. Lost in his many incarnations, for example, is that Stoker's Count could transform himself into mist and go outside *in daylight* so long as he wore a giant, floppy sun hat.

I learned about the Draculae in reverse of the usual order. Most people have the *Dracula* novel thrust into their hands by some well-meaning literature instructor in high school or university and later become vaguely aware that the Count is actually based on a real-life 15th-century prince/warlord/social deviant. I didn't read the novel, however, until my early 40s, long after I'd crisscrossed Romania to research sites associated with Vlad III Dracula for Lonely Planet guidebooks. Knowing that the real-life Dracula was infinitely more cunning, cruel and deadly than a fictional, supernatural monster was both sobering and fascinating.

I've visited plenty of legendary and notorious sites across Europe in my travels, but in Vlad's case my imagination was piqued not only by the number of surviving hangouts, but also by the captivating legend of this alternately courageous and brutal dude. Strolling over territory where unimaginable atrocities were committed, I'd speculate "I wonder if he impaled a guy *right here*? Or cut off some guy's nose to add to his obscene collection of facial parts over there?" My mind swirled.

Compared to Vlad's exploits, intrigues and triumphs, Count Dracula was a bit of an underachieving drag. All those supernatural powers and he couldn't at least, say, punch a hole through a guy's chest, yank out his still-beating heart and play a little keep-away with it till the guy collapsed? Show some enthusiasm for your art, man!

Despite that lack of graphic gore, *Dracula* has nevertheless inspired nearly 120 years of vampires getting their toothy freak on in books, theater, film and television. A sustained vampire cult orgasm that started with Anne Rice's 1976 novel *Interview with the Vampire* and effectively gasped to an ungraceful end (at least for a while) with 2012's *The Twilight Saga: Breaking Dawn – Part 2* has inspired more recovering-goth fashion remorse and made more people rich than all other classic supernatural creatures combined[3]. As way of proof, I'd like to point out that the

---

[3] Don't fact check that. Just take my word for it.

original *Dracula* novel, which is not exactly a literary thrill ride, has never been out of print. Nearly 120 years. Whoa.

The third player in my cabaret of enthrallment is Romania itself. This equally ill-fated and self-destructive nation at the eastern edge of Europe has made dramatic strides in the 12 years since I first set foot within its borders and is almost unrecognizable as the nation that spent years under hated dictator Nicolae Ceauşescu and his communist acolytes. And yet, despite being an excellent value destination and home to some of Europe's best natural attractions, it still suffers alternately from near-anonymity, tourism-wise, and as a go-to scapegoat for everything from Europe's economic problems to every kid who's ever picked a pocket in Rome. To drive my point home about Romania's tourism obscurity, the country's far and away most popular tourism region, Transylvania, has been name-checked in so many pieces of fictional literature, TV and film that people often mistakenly think it's a make-believe place, like Neverland.

Between my many trips to Romania, including living there in noncontiguous chunks between 2004 and 2006, I've spent more than two cumulative years on that storied soil, some days marveling at its near infinite tourism potential and others cursing whatever jerkface official had most recently screwed with me for the pure joy of screwing with me. It's an experiential and emotional rollercoaster, depending on fate and your proximity to bureaucratic, profiteering douchebags, as one Anthony Bourdain learned during his doomed visit to shoot an episode of his show "No Reservations" in 2008. He hasn't been back since[4]. Even the more affable Andrew Zimmern has avoided Romania thus far, choosing instead to take his "Bizarre Foods" crew to the—I'm sorry—*vastly* less fascinating country of Hungary in 2010[5].

In short, aside from its cartoonishly bad political theater and lazily concealed corruption, Romania is overdue for a PR win and I want to contribute to that effort.

To that end, in this book we shall be backpacking the Draculae trail together, so to speak. We will visit surviving sites associated with Vlad Dracula across the country, including Poenari Castle (the *real* Dracula's castle), his Princely Court at Târgovişte, his childhood home (now a restaurant) in Sighişoara, and more.

As a nod to Count Dracula's artificially introduced legacy in Romania, we shall also visit the Borgo Pass, the site of the fictional Castle Dracula where some entrepreneur has opened the kitschy Hotel Castel Dracula (sic), visit the campy Count Dracula Club in Bucharest, and take a close look at the Count's impact on Romania tourism, such as it is, including the oft-planned, delayed, and mercifully cancelled "Dracula Land" theme park.

---

[4] More on that in the Bucharest chapter.
[5] I know of this development because I briefly consulted with his producer about possible Romania activities in the early stages of selecting destinations for that season.

Finally, if I'm being completely frank, my Step Zero for writing this book was because, goddammit, I wanted to publish a book! I've had *three* perfectly good book proposals tragically die on the vine over the years due to bad timing, bad economy and bad representation. It was the ego-snuffing equivalent of taking, and barely surviving, three rides in a car compactor. I desperately wanted to cut that last key for my jangling ring of travel writer cred. So, I took two irresistible hooks, goofball humor, and an eternally saleable subject, and put them together.

That's how it's done.

Leif Pettersen
Minneapolis, 2016

# Sighişoara – A Star Is Born

We'll get to the mind-bending mountain ranges, Gothic castles, fortified towns, dusty peasant villages, striking moonlight and cabaret of shape-shifting, face-chomping monsters with prominent overbites in due course. First I need to begin by sharing the backstory of our headliner: Vlad III, Prince of Wallachia, a.k.a. Vlad Dracula, a.k.a. Vlad Ţepeş, a.k.a. "No, God, nooooooo!" to those who irritated him.

You'd be hard-pressed to find anyone who couldn't identify the elusive vampire protagonist in the novel *Dracula*, but few people are more than vaguely aware that the Count was loosely based on the real-life Vlad Dracula, 15th-century *voivode*[6] of Wallachia. He inherited the posthumous nickname "Ţepeş" (The Impaler) for his preferred method of drastically shortening the remainder of his enemies' lives with a sharpened piece of wood. The Ottomans, who grew to develop a healthy respect for Vlad's stake-wielding enthusiasm, took to calling him "*Kazıklı Bey*" (Sir Impaler).

When the character Marsellus Wallace uttered the exquisitely quotable phrase "I'mma get medieval on yo' ass" in the 1994 film *Pulp Fiction*, he was likely referring to Vlad's handiwork. History has rarely given us such a

---

[6] A Slavic catch-all term usually meaning "prince," but also "commander" or "warlord."

complex, paradoxical and memorable figure, whose sometimes hazily documented life was defined by so much violence and death that an Irish novelist reinvented him as a toothy undead predator more than four centuries later.

It goes without saying that the 15th century was a very different time, with morals that we'd consider shocking. Violence and the murder of whole families were legitimate ways to solve problems that would barely warrant a morning in small claims court today. This was particularly true for someone with a tenuous grip on a royal title in a territory surrounded by powerful entities smacking their lips over the thought of doing a bit of annexing. What we'd consider horrific war crimes were standard operating procedure for protecting one's land. Double goes for marching off to take someone else's.

And amid one of humanity's most ethically deficient periods, Vlad III Dracula was deemed a psychopath. That's no mean feat. How did that happen? In order to illustrate the complete picture of Dracula's life and the desperate, nearly impossible situation in which he found himself as Prince of Wallachia, we need to back up a couple of generations and set the scene starting with his grandfather, Mircea the Old[7].

------------------------------

Voivode Mircea, with some political squabbling-induced interruptions, ruled Wallachia for a whopping 32 years

---

[7] A.k.a. Mircea the Great.

between 1386 and 1418, an almost unthinkably long reign for the period[8]. Mircea spent much of his rule expanding Wallachia to roughly the shape we know it today. As principalities in the era went, it was admirably large and prosperous, but it was a veritable grape waiting to be eaten (or squished) compared to the strength of its two superpower neighbors of the time—the Hungarians to the northwest (and just beyond them, the Holy Roman Empire) and the Ottomans to the south. As such, Mircea devoted much of his time and resources into fortifying defenses against these entities.

Despite these efforts, Mircea eventually found himself faced with the choice of submission or probable annihilation after the Ottomans thrashed Bulgaria and camped out on Wallachia's doorstep along the Danube River. In 1393, Mircea signed Wallachia's first of many compliance agreements with Ottoman sultans, in this case Bayezid. Mircea's shame at the quick surrender only lasted until 1395, when he aligned himself with Holy Roman Emperor Sigismund of Luxembourg, a deal that included an insurance policy of Mircea's loyalty in the form of his son, little Vlad II, being sent to Buda[9] as a kind of study-abroad/hostage arrangement.

Along with a patchwork group of forces from all over Europe, Mircea joined a crusade against the Ottomans the

---

[8] In contrast, as you'll see, Vlad Dracula ruled for only seven cumulative, albeit wildly industrious, years.
[9] Now Budapest.

following year. This alliance was soon defeated, though Mircea and Wallachia were spared a punitive Turkish spanking when Tamerlane and his forces charged out of Asia Minor, requiring Sultan Bayezid to throw everything he had at his eastern front. The epic battle left Bayezid dead[10] and the Turks weakened, and in the ensuing internal power struggle Mircea's betrayal was essentially forgotten—for a time.

Mircea died in 1418, before the Turks had pulled themselves together enough to consider another run at Wallachia. The task of coping with that epic panic attack fell to his son, Vlad II.

Vlad II didn't inherit the title of Prince of Wallachia until many years after his father's death. And by "inherit," I mean of course dispense with numerous covetous siblings. Mircea, that slut, had fathered a small army of illegitimate children[11], all of whom believed they had rightful claim to the throne. Vlad II's half-brother Alexandru Aldea eventually succeeded in securing the position. Emperor Sigismund, who acted as a sort of semi-present father figure

---

[10] By suicide in captivity, somehow. I have $10 that says he invented strangulation by shoelaces.

[11] Romanian princes of the era had adopted the "harem philosophy" of the Ottomans, meaning there was no dishonor in having as many concubines as they could afford to support in addition to their legal wives. Any sons born of these concubines were thus equal heirs to any inheritance, including royal title, as "legitimate" sons. To use a delightful expression of the time, all that was required to inherit a royal title was that the son had come from "the male royal bone." Thus, when a prince died, all hell frequently broke loose between the assortment of half-brothers gunning for the throne.

and mentor while little Vlad II was raised, educated and
trained in his court, declined to help Vlad II take the throne
by force, but as a consolation prize awarded him the position
of military governor of Transylvania, which included a fancy
home in Sighișoara. Vlad II moved there with his family in
1431 to perform his duties, using his free time to exert his
claim on the throne.

Before sending Vlad II on his way, Emperor Sigismund
locked down their relationship (read: Vlad II's loyalty) by
inducting him into the chivalric Order of the Dragon.
Joining the order, which was founded in 1408 to promote
and protect Christianity in Eastern Europe, meant that Vlad
II had to convert to Catholicism from his native Orthodoxy[12].
While leaving the Orthodox Church would affect his
popularity back in Wallachia down the road[13], the religious
conversion was understandable. By that time, Vlad II had
spent a significant portion of his life in the West[14] under the
watch of Sigismund. Respecting his rather high rank back in
Wallachia, Sigismund gave Vlad II the sophisticated and
cosmopolitan education worthy of royalty. This long period
spent in the West, exposed to a doubtlessly Christian-
leaning education, must have made the conversion to

---

[12] Dracula would also convert to Catholicism, eventually.
[13] And the move likely confused the heck out of little Dracula, who at a
young age had the unenviable task of wondering why his father was
Catholic while everyone else in Romania was Orthodox. Dracula would
later face a similar conflict, as being Orthodox was virtually de rigueur
for princes of Wallachia.
[14] He's believed to have lived in Buda, spent time in various German
cities and visited Prague and Rome among other places.

Catholicism seem perfectly normal. Sigismund also bestowed Vlad II with the surname "Dracul" (from the Latin "draco," meaning "dragon").

Soon after arriving in Sighişoara in 1431, the Dracul family had a son. In a clear effort to someday make researching and writing a book like this a goddamn pain in the ass for some poor bastard[15], Vlad II gave this soon-to-be-infamous son his first name, Vlad (III), plus the Romanian name "Draculea"—literally "son of Dracul.[16]"

-----------------------------------------

Situated on the Târnava Mare River in central Transylvania, and very nearly in the smack-bang center of modern Romania itself, Sighişoara is the best-preserved fortified citadel (town) in the country, not to mention among the best in all of Europe. It is consequently one of the most popular tourist sites in Romania and thus many of its 28,102 inhabitants[17] work in tourism or the service industry.

"Sighie," as locals call it today, was one of the settlement hotspots for craftsmen, merchants and probably more than a few misunderstood, ex-military, Mad Max-like vagabonds when the King of Hungary encouraged people to relocate to Transylvania in the 12th century. With incursions

----

[15] Buy me a drink sometime, step back out of reasonable spittle flying distance, then ask me about keeping four or five 'Vlad's, three 'Dan's and a scattering of other shared-named people straight while combining material from several sources to write this book. Oh, it's hilarious.

[16] Bram Stoker would later choose to adopt the now famously misinterpreted meaning of the word "draco" (dragon), which, conveniently for him, was "devil."

[17] 2011 census.

and land-grabbing an ever-present threat, the king became preoccupied with locking down the distant and shakily controlled southeastern edge of his realm. As one does when one is fortifying new territory, the king offered tantalizing benefits and free land, never mind who was presently on it, to those willing to slum it in a grungy provincial outpost, getting a foothold in the region, developing its economy and, inevitably, defending it from the invaders-of-the-week.

The influx of colonists continued until the end of the 13th century. Though many of these expats were actually from western, Franconian-speaking Europe, the people who settled in Sighişoara are nonetheless referred to as "German Saxons," as this ethnic administered the region and reported to the Hungarian Chancellery. Historic documents suggest a noteworthy Saxon settlement existed in present-day Sighişoara by 1191.

By 1280 records indicate that a substantial, fortified town was taking shape, built on the site of an old asymmetrical hexagon-shaped Roman fort, which likely dated back to several hundred years BC. By 1337, Sighişoara had become a hangout for the rich, royal and all manner of poseurs—like a modern-day Brooklyn, but with super-crazy facial hair that you would not *believe* was ever considered fashionab... Oh. Never mind.

Wealth pooled in Sighişoara due to its position as a strategic and commercial center for the region, fueling development that made it one of Transylvania's most important cities. It was during this time that the 14th-century walls, which are still standing today, were completed. These walls were later reinforced with 14 towers and five artillery bastions, which stored ammunition, food and supplies and were outfitted with openings for firing cannon shells and arrows. Nine of these original towers, each named for the guild that maintained and defended it and two bastions are still intact.

By the 16th and 17th centuries, Sighişoara was supporting some 15 guilds and 20 handicraft branches. The loose cash and substantial bourgeoisie attracted artisans and craftsmen from around the Holy Roman Empire, particularly the continually arriving "German Saxons" who drove the town's economy and development. Sighişoara's guilds like the blacksmiths, butchers, cobblers, goldsmiths, tailors, carpenters and tinsmiths—only the latter four were allowed to have their workshops inside the citadel— remained an active and economically vital part of the civic architecture until 1875.

The 15th century ushered in one of Sighişoara's most famous residents, our hero Vlad III Dracula. Because apparently no one could keep their pants zipped for long in his heyday, Dracula is believed to be an illegitimate child. The identity of his true mother is unknown, but Dracula was raised by Vlad II's then-wife Princess Cneajna, eldest daughter of Alexander "the Good," Prince of Moldavia, and aunt to the future illustrious leader, warrior and eventual saint Stephen the Great of Moldavia, Dracula's first cousin, whose name will come up again later.

Though Dracula left Sighişoara with his family while he was still a toddler, the city proudly claims the future impaling ninja/wizard/guru/Jedi as its own. The house where little Vlad went through the teething process and likely learned the proper stance for delivering a powerful stabbing motion, though much altered, still stands today—as a restaurant. Aside from various tributes to Dracula himself, his association with the town has encouraged a modest gore and horror element among the tourism attractions, namely the Torture Museum and a collection of painful-looking, tetanus-delivering medieval arms.

Despite Hungary's unifying efforts, Sighişoara, along with the rest of Transylvania, eventually spent centuries functioning autonomously, but paying "tributes" and bowing down to the Ottomans. Even with benevolent Ottoman protection, the tempting power and tactical importance of the city nonetheless attracted repeated military occupations, along with the normal dangers of urban living during that time such as plagues and the odd devastating fire.

The seemingly never-ending encumbrance of unwanted, seesawing rule between the Turks and Austria-Hungary finally came to an end at the conclusion of World War I when the keys to Sighişoara, along with all of Transylvania, were handed over to the Kingdom of Romania.

-------------------------------------

Sighişoara is a UNESCO World Heritage Site. A lengthy and comprehensive restoration of the citadel's historic fortifications, structures, houses, and streets in the mid-

2000s undid more than a century of neglect. These days central Sighişoara is a gorgeous, tourist-besieged living museum of a small, medieval fortified city. Some would argue it's the finest inhabited citadel in all of Europe. Outside the fortifications, the "lower town," which dips into the Târnava Mare river valley, is a little less hectic and also quite pretty. Depending on your perspective, the city is best visited or avoided during the over-the-top Medieval Festival held annually in late July, featuring unintentionally amusing costumes, parades, dances and staged battles.

Well-to-do medieval craftsmen owned the houses inside the citadel, for the most part, and, though heavily refurbished, the structures are virtually the same now as they were during Sighişoara's heyday. It's said many of these coveted, ancient homes were acquired by their current owners via dubious circumstances during communist times, though some are still occupied by descendents of families that have called Sighişoara home for centuries. Naturally, several operate as small B&Bs and, last time I checked, spending the night in one of these homes was reasonably affordable. The same cannot be said of the cluster of hotels around the town squares, which are unquestionably lovely, but ambitiously priced.

The ethnic German community, though diminutive, remains a presence in Sighişoara, numbering roughly 500. It's this tiny foothold and historic nostalgia that pulled in the largely German-sourced funding for Sighie's top-to-bottom restoration.

Sighişoara narrowly avoided going over to the Dark Side of shameless tourist bait when a collection of halfwits with euro signs for irises started pushing ahead with plans to build "Dracula Land."

The worrying concept for this cheapening of Romania, the Count, and the Prince (and, probably, theme parks) started circulating in the early 2000s. Initially, the park was going to be placed just outside Sighişoara. This proposed site was met with powerful opposition from local officials, environmentalists[18], and even Prince Charles, whose distant Romanian ancestry has made him a de facto Romania cheerleader and outspoken cultural preservationist. The project would have included a massive, heinous mock castle looming over Sighisoara's exceptionally well-preserved medieval citadel. The chimes of the 13th-century clock tower would have been drowned out by the din of rollercoasters and arcade games drifting down the hill. In a rare instance of well-funded shortsightedness being defeated by civic conviction in Romania, with the added glare of outrage shined on the proposal by national and international media, Dracula Land was scrapped before a single ancient oak tree could be bulldozed.

Frustrated tourism officials, arguing that the park's one million annual visitors could potentially double Romania's pitiable tourism sector revenue, vowed to find an alternative site.

---

[18] Construction would require mowing down an ancient oak tree reserve.

Soon the proposed project was revived on a site north of Bucharest, near Snagov Monastery[19], where Vlad Dracula was formerly believed to have been buried. Unable to attract enough investors to pony up the $15.6 million needed for construction, tourism officials dropped the plan entirely.

Even without that atrocity, Sighişoara remains a relentless bus-tour disgorging point, yet spending the night, never mind a couple nights, in Sighişoara doesn't appear on many itineraries. Thus, like visitors to Venice or Mont Saint-Michel, people who hang around after the tour buses roar away will be rewarded with a mellow(er) evening of strolling down half-a-millennium-old, hilly, cobblestone lanes, through minor squares, down winding alleys, up sharp stairways, and around pastel-colored structures while entertaining whatever fantasies one's imagination conjures.

When you've had your fill of that distraction, locate one of the city's hard-to-find good meals or just get to drinking wine on the cobblestones of a centuries-old square.

----------------------------------------

I've lost count of how many times I've been to Sighie for both guidebook research and pleasure trips. It's a comparatively chilled out stop between the commotion of Braşov and Sibiu, the other two corners of the so-called "Transylvanian Triangle." Plus, being so compact, it's mercifully easy on a guidebook researcher's abused feet.

---

[19] Which we'll get to later, because boy did that place see some drama!

My first trip there was pre-restoration, when the citadel's crumbling buildings and dilapidated, ankle-breaking cobblestones gave it a sad, shabby-chic quality.

Now the hilly cobblestone streets are immaculate and the brightly colored houses are movie-backdrop-ready. Bells clang from a half dozen or so tightly clustered churches, sidewalk exhibits share space with café patios in front of artisan shops, and tour groups shuffle around, led by guides shouting in a dozen languages. And there is no shortage of opportunities to acquire Dracula T-shirts, handicrafts of dubious merit and locally made țuică[20] in gaudy souvenir bottles shaped like castles and bears and whatnot.

It sounds tackier than it is, though I know some of my finicky guidebook-writing cohorts find Sighişoara's passionate, tongue-kissing embrace of mass tourism off-putting considering the otherwise informal, somehow charmingly disinterested state of the tourism industry in other Romanian cities.

No matter what your feelings are on day-trip, tourist-bait sights, there's no arguing that Sighie is an authentic, full-sensory medieval experience. The partial vehicle restriction in the citadel adds to this enchantment, allowing one to safely stagger around in a distracted, Instagram-snapping daze without fear of flattened toes.

---

[20] Homemade brandy, usually made from plums, but also sometimes apples, grapes, and other fruits.

Most first-time visitors will (and should) enter Sighişoara's citadel by passing through the tunnel under the massive clock tower (*Turnul cu Ceas*). It's easy to see this was once the citadel's main entrance and though there are innumerable entry points in the walls today, it's still the ideal way to enter Sighişoara for maximum drama. The tower dates from 1280 and is an impressive 64 meters (209 feet) tall, topped by a main spire that is surrounded by four baby spires, and anchored by a sturdy base with walls 2.35 meters (7.7 feet) thick, which must have been a real headache for medieval banditos intent on doing a little sacking.

The tower's exterior features several rows of what are now windows, but must have formerly been offensive portals with all manner of cannons and crossbows poking out. On both the Lower Town-facing and citadel-facing sides of the tower, about four-fifths of the way up the decaying mortar-covered brick façade are clocks dating from 1648. The clocks house rudimentary, mechanical 2.5-foot wood-carved characters from the Greek-Roman pantheon, which trundle out along with figurines representing the days of the week during hourly routines. It's all very quaint, but honestly the up-close view of the grinding cogs, rings and rods that drive the figurines' movements inside the Clock Tower is far more entrancing.

The spacious, multi-floored interior of the Clock Tower once housed the town council. Today it's a wonderful History Museum, with a variety of small rooms and displays winding up to the 7th-floor outdoor viewing deck, which looks over both the citadel and the Lower Town streets, still lined with 16th-century tile-roofed Saxon houses. Keep an eye out for the gingerbread wood blocks, which the locals were using as far back as 1376[21].

Arguably the most arresting display is on the first level, featuring a small exhibition on modern Romanian hero, and brief, prepubescent Sighişoara resident, Hermann Oberth (June 25, 1894 – December 28, 1989).

Oberth was an ethnic German Saxon physicist and engineer born in nearby Sibiu and is considered one of the founding fathers of rocketry and astronautics. Oberth started doodling and contemplating space rockets at the age of 14. While studying medicine and physics in Munich he went on a publishing tear, pondering at great length various facets of theoretical space travel which, naturally, was roundly dismissed by the scientific community as lunacy.

In 1929 he left a trail of circular, burnt patches of grass in his wake as he began testing liquid-fueled rocket motors. That same year, his rocket designs were used wholesale to build the model spaceships featured in the shoestring-budgeted, fairly popular Fritz Lang film *Woman on the Moon*. One presumes this film was exhaustively screened by Germany's transfixed senior military commanders, because soon after its release the army giddily fast-tracked a rocket-research program, recruiting Oberth

---

[21] The display models date from the 18th-century.

and several members of the same nay-saying, now crow-eating scientific community.

During WWII, Oberth co-developed Nazi Germany's infamous V-2 rocket, the first long-range, guided ballistic missile in the world. Amazingly, Oberth somehow emerged from the war free of Axis obligation and Allied retribution and continued to build on his work, writing the 1953 book *Menschen im Weltraum* (Man into Space), in which he made detailed descriptions of theoretical space-based reflecting telescopes, space stations, electric-powered spaceships, and space suits. His work took him from Nazi Germany to Switzerland, Italy, the U.S., and then back to a free Germany. Oberth worked for NASA and was present for the launching of both the 1969 Apollo 11 moon mission and the space shuttle Challenger in 1985. Despite living in Sighişoara for only a few years as a child, officials nonetheless renamed the central square in Lower Town Hermann Oberth Square.

The limited displays in the Sighişoara museum adequately feature some of Oberth's accomplishments, including a bold, yet in retrospect naïve sketch of his rudimentary space suit, but if you find yourself craving a more comprehensive biographical summary of his life's work, seek out the Hermann Oberth Space Museum near Nuremberg, Germany.

------------------------------

It's deviously under-advertised, but Sighie has a combo ticket for reduced entrance to the Clock Tower/History Museum and two others:

Under the clock tower, down some stairs is the first bonus attraction, a small, dark and spookily dank Torture Room Museum. If you've traveled much in Europe, you know "torture museums" are a dime a dozen, more campy horror show than museum, usually filled with fake devices, disemboweled mannequins and the occasional motion-activated, jump-up, screaming skeleton. Screw those. This one's legit.

Prisoners were actually tortured for "confessions" down in this hellhole. On display are authentic devices for crushing fingers and inflicting burns with red-hot coals, as well as the foot-squishing "Spanish boot." That said, it's small and quickly absorbed, which often leaves stone-hearted, less imaginative visitors feeling underwhelmed and overcharged[22].

Just inside the citadel is Piaţa Muzeului (Museum Square), the subject of about 90 percent of the photos you'll see in a "Sighişoara" search of Google images. Here you'll find the third combo-ticket attraction, a small collection of medieval arms. Four rooms are filled with genuine medieval helmets, shields, cross-bows, maces (labeled "whips for fight") and cannonballs. The seemingly out-of-place drawing of Napoleon in here complements a painting of Michael

---

[22] Thus the combo ticket recommendation.

Freiherr von Melas (1731-1806), a Sighişoara native who, while a general of the Austrian mounted troops, fought against Napoleon Bonaparte's army at Marengo in 1800. This, too, is not an especially large exhibit, but combined with the Torture Room Museum and the Clock Tower/History Museum, the combo ticket offers a solid hour of good-value, worthwhile distraction.

On the opposite side of Piaţa Muzeului is the Gothic-style Church of the Dominican Monastery (*Biserica Manastirii*; 1556). Behind *that*, on a pedestal in the center of an unassuming but lovely cobblestone square, is a rudimentary, stone-chiseled bust of Vlad Dracula. Why this perfect Dracula selfie opportunity is hidden back here where only guidebook authors would think to snoop, I have no idea. In a rare show of artistic restraint, this particular rendering of Dracula doesn't include the customary furious facial expression, the one that suggests he's contemplating removing the eyeballs of an ingrate aristocrat with a wooden spoon.

Back in Piaţa Muzeului is Sighişoara's main Dracula attraction, the house where he was born in 1431. The three-level house is impressively spacious, made from stone and wood, mustard yellow, with a tiled roof. All three entrances face the square, and eight standard windows decorate the second and third levels. The ground floor has only one tiny window, a defensive precaution common during the era due to frequent street scuffles and melees breaking out in lieu of diplomatic solutions to things like someone's dog pooping in someone else's yard—or so I have idly imagined. A plaque posted above and to the right of the door, written in Romanian, explains that Vlad II Dracul, son of Mircea the Old, lived in the house from 1431 to 1435[23].

Some sources say this house may have been much smaller in Dracula's time, maybe just a single story, but knowing Vlad II's wealth and hereditary station, this seems unlikely. Furthermore, as Vlad II was military governor of Transylvania, he would have almost certainly been put up in style. The residence would have needed to be large enough to house the garrison assigned to Vlad II[24], with enough space left for his family as well as the modest court where he conducted business. The house was restored in 1976 and again in the early 2000s, as part of Sighişoara's comprehensive facelift.

Little Dracula left this house, and Sighişoara, at the age of four with his family and moved to Wallachia when Vlad II Dracul took the throne. The large, three-level structure now houses a restaurant, opportunistically named "Casa Dracula." Visitors can thus freely walk in the door, linger and absorb the centuries-old, pre-impaling Dracula essence in the structure. Having processed that dubious sensation, go ahead and have a drink here (red wine, presumably) or even a meal. At last pass the prices were fair and the food was decent though unremarkable.

---

[23] Paraphrased.
[24] They were likely living on the ground floor.

A few paces deeper into the citadel brings you to the much larger Piaţa Cetatii (Fortress Square), the civic and communal hub of the citadel. Back in impaling times, this is where Sighişoara held its markets, fairs, more than a few no-doubt lively witch trials, and swift public executions. These days it serves many of the same functions, lack of witch-busting notwithstanding. The square is ringed by white and pastel-colored three-story buildings, a few of which seem to have been passed over during the restoration work of the previous decade, identifiable by their crumbling façades and ad hoc patch work. The square is all artisan shops, café and restaurant patios and, disappointingly, parking for guests of the citadel's pricey hotels. Still, even while staring into the hood and headlights of a Citroën, it is somehow atmospheric and an appropriate place for libations.

Once every corner of these central squares has been absorbed, the last item on the top-shelf Sighişoara agenda is to stroll the perimeter of the citadel walls, passing the surviving nine towers and two bastions as well as a number of ancient and awe-inspiring churches that probably deserve a hell of a lot more than a fleeting mention in a single sentence like I just did. I will go into detail about one, though.

Southeast of Piaţa Cetatii, at the end of the uphill and inviting Strata Scolii, one finds a set of covered steps—172 of them. Originally built in 1642, they lead up to the Church on the Hill, which dates from 1345. This sturdy Lutheran church is not only an incredible, ancient Gothic edifice housing 500-year-old frescoes, but it also occupies the town's highest point, providing some great photo ops of the area down below. Nearby is a moody, wild German cemetery.

--------------------------------------

After three or four visits to Sighie in as many years for Lonely Planet guidebook research, my author anonymity in town was pretty much blown. Like Braşov, Suceava, and Sibiu, Sighişoara was one of only a handful of Romanian destinations where people understood, cared about or had even heard of Lonely Planet and the power of a listing therein.

In a few cases, getting into and maintaining an LP listing drove people in Romanian tourism to maniacal, creepy lengths. Judging by cumulative evidence, in my later guidebook-researching years, as soon as I landed in Romania, phone lines and email accounts among a small group of individuals would light up and presumably keep open channels about my whereabouts and progress through the country. One time a hostel owner somehow tracked down and called my cellphone within a few days of my arrival, even though it was a new SIM card and phone number that only two or three people in the world knew about. I mean, I'm *pretty* sure Romania's dreaded Securitate[25] are done and gone, but that was some freaky espionage right there. So, while I spent much of my time in Romania

---

[25] Communist-era secret police.

begging indifferent hotel clerks to let me inspect rooms or being interrogated by paranoid restaurant servers and train station ticket agents after asking one too many questions, I also become a bit unwound over the unsettling stalking factor.

Being an outed LP author in a lucrative tourist destination presents a variety of problems (e.g., duplicity and sabotage between business owners, and having to work extra-hard to uncover the everyday tourist experiences in a hostel, hotel or restaurant when one is being treated like royalty). There are some refreshing advantages, though, namely: fleeting, desperately needed camaraderie.

Being on the road alone for four to six weeks, usually working 10-14 hours a day, seven days a week is more than a little wearying and lonely. Pulling into a place where you can spend some time with familiar faces, and in some cases good friends, goes a long way toward maintaining sanity on research trips.

Sighişoara was one of those places. Among my friendly acquaintances in town was the owner of a now-closed hostel outside of the citadel, a man I'll call "Tom." Like pretty much everyone in Romania, Tom had relatives living out in the countryside who produced their own ţuica. Ţuica quality ranges from grappa-caliber excellence to ear-smoking, hair-melting, speedboat paint remover. Tom's ţuica was the former and he always had a bottle stashed away with my name on it. My visits to Sighişoara would usually include a rare planned day off, just so I could stay up late indulging in țuica and good company and then do absolutely nothing the next day except gorge on Romania's reputed hangover-remedy dishes[26].

Inside the citadel, a sweet family owned a couple of beautifully restored, adjacent medieval homes that they'd converted into one of my favorite B&Bs. Without a family legacy in town, I wasn't sure how they had acquired *two* of these coveted houses and I didn't wanna know. They were friendly and doted on their guests and that's all I cared about. Moreover, their prices were surprisingly low, considering that other B&Bs were charging more to stay in much shabbier rooms.

When doing LP research, most of the time I was all business. I walked directly and swiftly from one objective to another, got the information I needed, then hauled ass to the next thing. Only rarely and in select places did I allow myself to just lollygag and kind of meander down random streets, and Sighişoara was one of those places. Like Salzburg or Venice, much of the appeal of Sighişoara is simply *being* in Sighişoara, absorbing the time-travel vibe and letting one's imagination run wild. With the environs so well preserved, you don't need to work very hard to imagine what life was like in Sighişoara 100, 250 and 500 years ago.

Walking down streets unchanged for centuries, I liked to picture the untold thousands, perhaps millions, of people

---

[26] The most famous of these is *ciorba de burta* (a sour cream and vinegar-based tripe soup). I shall refrain from comment and let you test this remedy yourself.

who had walked the exact same route spanning half a millennium. I'd touch the ancient walls, buildings and churches and wonder exactly when those stones had been placed there, how many other people had touched them and, inevitably, how many drunk dudes had peed on them.

The other reason Sighişoara serves as ideal wandering grounds is, as I mentioned before, it's small enough that even a comprehensive exploration of the citadel takes only an hour or so. After you've walked something like 15 miles every day for a few weeks, you learn to cherish the stops in compact towns where even an end-to-end crossing on foot takes just five minutes.

Sighişoara is also one of the few places where I toured all the museums pretty much every year, even if nothing had changed—an extravagance other veteran guidebook authors will confirm is rare and precious. When a given point-of-interest (POI) hasn't gone through any significant changes since your last visit, the normal operating procedure is to walk in, confirm prices and hours, and get the hell back on the road so you can devote appropriate time to the POIs that *have* changed since your last research visit.

Naturally, sooner or later one needs a break from the crowds, or just a decent meal, so one must exit the citadel and descend into Lower Town. There are, of course, little pockets of decent food hidden in the corners of the citadel, which are just fine if you don't mind paying a bit more. Otherwise, the food in Lower Town has always been superior, not to mention less expensive. And here's the thing: oddly, there aren't that many restaurants in Sighișoara. If one or two people with some genuine cooking skills set up shop in town, they'd make a killing. Still, there are good meals to be had, though I won't go into detail, since it's been too long since my last visit and eating recommendations are among the first things in guidebooks to go stale.

OK fine, I'll mention one place: Rustic, on Strada 1 Decembrie 1918, which still exists if Google Street View can be trusted, was my go-to place for most meals, particularly the mornings after a little too much fun at Tom's hostel. It's just simple, no-nonsense Romanian food, but that's exactly what one needs some days, particularly on a guidebook author's budget and the average meal at Rustic costing about seven bucks. Go there, hangover or no.

Though I've never had to deal with this personally, I know from research that getting to or from Sighișoara on public transportation, especially the bus, is a bit more challenging than most tourist sites in Transylvania. There's service, of course, but it's not as frequent as you'd hope and often requires a transfer at some stage. So bring a book, a snack, and watch the liquid intake, as bathrooms (or, more accurately, bathrooms that you'd be willing to use) will be few and far between on that long travel day.

---------------------------------------

People spending a few days in Sighișoara (hangover day notwithstanding, natch), or those on a truly epic day trip, will want to time-travel through one or more of the nearly two hundred 13th and 15th-century Saxon villages in the area, which are arguably among the highlights of Saxon Transylvania. Seven fortified Saxon churches in these villages (Biertan, Calnic, Darjiu, Prejmer, Saschiz, Valea Viilor, and Viscri) have been designated as UNESCO World Heritage Sites and have enjoyed preservation and restoration, largely funded by the Mihai Eminescu Trust.

Public transport is thin in these parts, so you'll need a car, stout legs and a bike or a sense of humor, plus heroic patience for hitchhiking to traverse the rolling hills between the church towns[27].

Chief among these is Biertan, about 27 kilometers (17 miles) southwest of Sighişoara. Biertan's main attraction is its incredible triple-walled Saxon church, which may look familiar as it appears on the front of many guidebooks and postcards. The 15th-century church was the site of the Lutheran bishop from 1572 to 1867 and was therefore the beneficiary of suitable decoration and defensive measures.

For example, the immaculately maintained interior contains a massive, opulent Viennese-style altar (1483-1550) with 28 painted panels. For such a famous, heavily fortified church, the seating capacity isn't particularly large—maybe 150 people, max—which must incite a virtual scrum for those precious seats during the monthly services,

---

[27] And, assuming you're not in a hurry or starving, there are much worse places to get stuck on the side of the road for an hour.

particularly as no other fortified churches in the area have any kind of regular worship.

Biertan's church has three rings of exterior walls, standing up to 12 meters (39 feet) tall in places and connected by watchtowers and gates that provide cinematic views of the nearby rolling hills, ancient tile-roofed houses down in the village, and terraced vineyards.

Without question, the coolest artifact inside the church is the door of the sacristy, where the church's treasures were once stored. The door has 19 locks, all operated by a single locking mechanism, an ancient engineering triumph that won first prize at the Paris World Expo in 1900.

According to local legend, a small bastion on the church grounds was used for some 400 years as a last-ditch option for couples wanting a divorce. The estranged couple was locked in the bastion for two weeks with no choice but to communicate and work together as they were only furnished with one bed and one set of cutlery. Legend has it this method was so successful that only one couple decided to pursue divorce after their confinement in 400 years[28].

More difficult to reach, but just as popular, is the fortified church in Viscri, a tiny Saxon village about 42 kilometers (26 miles) southeast of Sighişoara that is known for having the affection of England's Prince Charles, who

---

[28] For all those other couples, the rest of their lives just *seemed* like 400 years, amirite?

claims Romanian antecedents and allegedly owns land in the area.

You may never want to leave this place; partly because it's so flipping cool and atmospheric and partly because, well, you might not be able to. Without any regularly scheduled visits by public transport (when last I checked), getting here without private transport means a bit of lucky hitchhiking and/or requires a shit-ton of walking. More so on the return trip to Sighişoara, being that the village itself is at the end of a busted-up road a long ways off the main thoroughfare. The upside of this remote, transportation-challenged oasis is things here are pricelessly quiet, allowing one to soak up the simple, quiet Saxon village beauty.

A wide, gently sloping dirt road serves as the village's main street. On either side are cement-covered, wooden houses painted in a variety of white and pastel colors, blue being far and away the most popular choice. Most houses are two stories[29] with clay-tiled roofs and giant wooden gates that lead to inner courtyards for parking one's cart and horses (and probably cars, but let's not ruin the atmosphere). Apart from a few parked cars, power lines and the occasional streetlight, there's nothing on this road to suggest which century you're in.

---

[29] Though, judging by the lack of windows, it appears the upper level is simply storage more often than not.

Since you went through the trouble to get here, you should spend the night. You can find a bunch of unmarked and unofficial pensions in lovely Saxon homes—most with pit toilets out in the garden, just so you know. People wanting full immersion will want to seek out one of the coveted 200-year-old "Saxon beds," oversized cabinets with enormous drawers that pull out to reveal mattresses! Fair warning: by the looks of them, sleeping in these things is more about the experience than a comfortable, sound night's sleep.

Aside from melting into village life, there is, of course, the fortified church, also a UNESCO World Heritage site, dating from 1185. For reasons that probably made sense in the 12th century, the church is several hundred yards down a dirt road out of town. It doesn't hold a candle to Biertan in terms of size, but Viscri's church has the requisite fortifications, which, to look at them, probably didn't overly inconvenience people determined to do some looting, but it's fortified nonetheless. Its defenses include thick walls more than 20 feet tall and several stout-looking watchtowers, perforated with tiny holes for firing arrows at Ottomans and such. The walls and towers are mainly made up of stone and brick covered in a smooth layer of cement, all of it painted white, though one section either never had or has since lost its cement coating and is simply exposed stone and brick. One of the towers, with the cement exterior slowly crumbling away, has clearly visible Latin inscriptions high up the wall. These begin with a date from the mid-17th century written in Roman numerals (the last number is indecipherable due to decay) and continue for a full paragraph.

Inside the fortifications, Viscri is comparatively snug. The church occupies most of the space, though there are areas set aside for living quarters and workspace. The church interior is also fairly small. During my last visit, the interior looked like it was overdue for some restoration, with some pews literally falling apart and some alarmingly rickety stairs leading to the balcony that I only climbed half way before I chickened out and turned around.

Viscri's church, as well as the churches in many of the smaller Saxon towns, is open sporadically and whimsically. If you find yourself standing at a locked church door, ask around the village for the caretaker to get entry.

# The Making of a Psychopath

After biding his time and performing a series of alliances, betrayals, hurt feelings, and a shitload of puncture wounds, Vlad II Dracul was successful in ousting and/or out-maneuvering the squadron of half-brothers vying for rule of Wallachia. Vlad II moved his family from Sighişoara to Târgovişte, the capital of Wallachia, and began in 1436 his first of two sittings on the throne.

Dracula had two older half-brothers, Mircea II and Vlad Călugărul, as well as a younger brother, Radu III. At Târgovişte, the boys were educated by Romanian and Greek scholars in subjects like geography, mathematics, science, languages, the classical arts, court etiquette, philosophy, and a variety of physical skills like swimming, fencing, jousting, archery, and horsemanship, the latter of which was Dracula's particular talent.

As with Dracula's later rule of Wallachia, Vlad II seemed to be perpetually embroiled in or caught between the dizzying political, military pivoting and "gotchas" of the period. Sigismund was still rending his clothing about Turkish forays into Wallachia and Transylvania, which had begun while Vlad II's half-brother Alexandru Aldea ruled Wallachia, something Dracul was probably expected to halt once he took the throne. But Emperor wishes in far-off Buda likely didn't carry much weight while one was staring into the face of overwhelming Turkish forces, which now controlled the entire length of the Bulgarian side of the Danube River as well as a few important fortresses on the Wallachian side. Like his father before him, Vlad II had little choice but to sign a treaty of submission to the Sultan and continue paying the annual tributes, which had begun during Mircea's rule.

Vlad II's first head-spinning, action-packed reign in Wallachia lasted six years. By 1442, his main backer in Buda, Emperor Sigismund, was dead, and having been reluctantly complicit in a murderous and destructive Ottoman incursion into Transylvania hadn't won him any new fans in Hungary. It was decided that someone needed to pay a visit to Dracul at his Princely Court in Târgoviște and talk some sense into him. Hungary sent in John Hunyadi.

Hunyadi is considered a hero to both Hungarians and Romanians today[30], but at the time he was an ambitious, power-hungry dude, willing to do whatever it took to get what he wanted. Hunyadi was self-educated, self-made, an old-school adventurer, popular with the ladies[31] and so fantastically wealthy *he* loaned money to the *Holy Roman Emperor*[32]. Exceptionally crusade-happy, he was resolute in driving the Turks out of Europe and ending their loitering outside Constantinople, threatening to conquer it. Naturally, Hunyadi would go on to play a huge role in the lives of both Vlad II Dracul and Vlad III Dracula. Having made his

---

[30] Interestingly, Hunyadi was an ethnic Romanian.
[31] He was well-known for his gifts on the dance floor.
[32] With interest.

fortune and switched his focus to acquiring political power, he had ascended to being Viceroy of Hungary and Voivode of Transylvania, with ambitions to rule all of Central and Eastern Europe.

Hunyadi was not able to convince Dracul to renew his loyalty to Christian Europe, mainly because Dracul knew it would mean the obliteration of Wallachia by the Turks. Dracul was likely also aware that Hunyadi was in cahoots with a rival in Transylvania, Basarab, son of one of Dracul's half-brothers, who still coveted the throne. Dracul ultimately decided to remain neutral.

But the poor guy was stuck between a rock and a hard sultan. Despite Dracul's albeit half-hearted show of loyalty, Sultan Murad wasn't convinced of his commitment to their treaty. Dracul was summoned to Gallipoli and immediately taken into custody. In a moment of mystifying naiveté, Dracul had somehow misread the situation and brought his sons Dracula and Radu along on the trip. The boys, Dracula 11 years old[33] and Radu just 7, were ferried away and locked up in a mountain fortress at Egrigöz, in Asia Minor. Back in Wallachia, Dracul's eldest son Mircea took the throne while his dad talked it out with Murad.

The phrase "in for a penny, in for a pound" (or something like it) must have been thrown around a lot in the 15th century. After a likely tense full year of being Murad's "guest," in 1443 Dracul was forced to swear his allegiance to

---

[33] Possibly 12.

the Sultan, again, on both the Bible and the Quran to cover all the bases. Only then was he set free to return to Wallachia, where he ultimately ruled for another four years.

Still not quite convinced that the "fickle" Dracul would keep to the agreement, Murad also demanded that Dracul send 500 boys from Wallachia to serve in the Turkish army. As a final guarantee of Dracul's allegiance, Murad decided to keep Dracula and Radu in his court for loyalty insurance, an arrangement that would last for six years. It wasn't a wholly unproductive six years, though. During the brothers' confinement, the Ottomans rather kindly continued their education and training. They studied logic, literature, the Quran, warfare, and horse riding. Dracula also eventually became fluent in the Turkish language, a skill that would prove highly useful later in life.

--------------------------------

The Ottomans, who by this stage had made alarming headway in eroding control of the Byzantine Empire, encroaching ever closer to Constantinople (today's Istanbul), had also locked down once mighty Bulgaria, Albania, and most of Serbia. With the Balkans all but lost and Vlad II Dracul now more closely tied to the Sultan than ever, there was virtually nothing keeping the Ottomans from marching across Wallachia and continuing their expansion into Christian Europe. So, basically, the opposite of what the beleaguered, politically whiplashed Dracul had originally set out to do.

Up in Transylvania, John Hunyadi had taken a short break from his political ambitions to attack Turkish forces that had made their way into his turf. Pope Eugenius IV, wanting to ride this momentum, belatedly declared the crusade to kick the Turks out of Europe once and for all, rallying Christian forces from Central and Eastern Europe, all led by Hunyadi.

More concerned for his sons' lives than ever, Dracul dared not join this crusade, though he quietly sent a small group of soldiers to assist, led by his son Mircea. This impressively prolific crusade managed to clear much of the Balkans of Ottoman forces, sweeping and gashing south and east all the way to Sofia before winter set in. With war being prohibitively unpleasant to wage in winter and their supplies running low, Hunyadi and his forces retreated to Belgrade to wait for spring.

After a brief armistice for the Sultan to presumably catch his breath, Christian forces broke the treaty and advanced once again on the Ottomans, led again by Hunyadi along with King Ladislas of Poland, his forces, and a combined Venetian-Burgundian fleet on the Bosporus strait to prevent Turkish boats from paddling through to assist.

Dracul was asked again to contribute soldiers, but the combination of his conscience, his captive sons, and the warnings from an oracle[34] caused Dracul to decline. While in

---

[34] Dracul, like many people from Romania and the region, was extremely superstitious.

these negotiations with Hunyadi and the Polish king, a concerned Dracul took note of the relatively small Christian army of roughly 15,000 and begged Hunyadi to abort, adding in a no-doubt exasperated tone that the Sultan goes hunting on the weekend with more men than that. Hunyadi ignored this plea. Nonetheless, Dracul once again sent in Mircea with a small group of Wallachian troops to support Polish and Hungarian forces.

Mircea's forces were successful in taking out a Turkish garrison at Petretz and tossing them all to their deaths in the moat, but that was about the only thing that went right. The Venetians and Burgundians failed to keep the Ottomans from crossing the Bosporus, and the Christian army, as Dracul predicted, was outnumbered three to one. The Ottomans pounded Hunyadi at the Battle of Varna, killing King Ladislas in the process. Hunyadi escaped by the skin of his teeth, but he was roundly blamed for the defeat. Mircea soon pressed for Hunyadi to be tried and executed for his incompetence. Hunyadi's cumulative efforts on behalf of Christian Europe in previous years and his overall popularity were likely key to his life being spared. He was allowed to return to Transylvania to lick his wounds.

Word had gotten back to the Sultan that Dracul had betrayed him by sending Mircea and Wallachian forces into the crusade. This development was also shared with Dracula, who was probably still more than a little cranky about having been abandoned by his father in Asia Minor and now ostensibly condemned to death thanks to his actions.

Vlad and Radu's futures looked even bleaker the following year (1445) when Dracul himself joined a last-gasp crusade up the Danube with a Burgundian fleet to recapture two of his fortresses and lay down a little payback for the Battle of Varna. Though the operation was successful, the Ottomans dug in and remained in control of the region.

Amazingly, Murad did not kill or blind Dracula and Radu, preferring instead to continue using them as psychological pawns against Dracul, though the circumstances of their confinement were almost certainly made harsher. Not that it mattered much at this stage—the damage to Dracula's psyche was likely already irreversible.

Being held captive by the Sultan had set young Dracula on course to becoming the most truculent, sullen teenager in all of 15th-century Europe. The emotional ramifications of being abandoned by his father aside, Dracula was captive in a foreign place with strange customs and surrounded by people who spoke an unfamiliar language. Even an amenable kid would likely get frustrated in such circumstances. As he grew older and more pissed off, Dracula became less of an agreeable hostage and was often punished for impertinence or rebellion. The cumulative years of his resistance and, in all likelihood, corporal punishment at the hands of the Ottomans were probably the key to his evolution from optimistic, talented youngster into a fierce, sadistic warrior with a special fondness for perforating Ottomans.

Meanwhile, Radu was earning points as a goodie-good brown-noser. His exemplary behavior and natural good looks soon earned him the nickname "*Radu cel Frumos*" (Radu the Handsome) from his charmed captors. As Dracula and Radu grew apart, Radu formed a friendship with the Sultan's son, Mehmed II, alienating and isolating Dracula further.

It wasn't all a cakewalk for Radu, however. When word got back to the court that their father Dracul had violated his agreement with the Sultan during the final crusade, Radu was punished with sexual assault inflicted by none other than his BFF, Mehmed. Though this incident can't have been great for their friendship, Radu must have gotten over it, as he later became the future Sultan's "companion," if you catch my drift.

As planned, Murad was able to manipulate Dracul by keeping his sons alive. Dracul accepted an appalling truce arrangement that included losing his recently re-acquired fortresses and lands during the Danube operation, handing over to the Turks 4,000 Bulgarians who had taken refuge in Wallachia, and finally sending 500 young Wallachian men to serve in the Ottoman army as janissaries[35].

---

[35] Effectively slave warriors. The Ottomans made a habit out of "recruiting" (more like kidnapping) the strongest, most promising young boys in the regions they had absorbed, converting them to Islam, training them, and sticking them in the Turkish infantry. Despite having been drafted against their will, troops that embraced their predicament

John Hunyadi, never a huge fan of Vlad II due to his reluctance to fight the Turks, and still righteously livid about Vlad II and Mircea's (rightly) blaming him for the whole Varna fiasco, resolved to punish the Prince for these renewed relations with the Ottomans. Having recruited Vladislav II of the Dăneşti clan[36] from Braşov as successor to the Wallachian throne (and devout ally), Hunyadi started a smear campaign to weaken Dracul in late 1447. He later rolled up to Târgovişte with Vladislav at his side to physically unseat Dracul. Though Dracul and Mircea had locked themselves up in the Princely Court, local boyars[37]

---

were eligible for promotion up the ranks all the way to prime minister to the sultan. This groundbreaking, cruel strategy left the conquered Ottoman territories perpetually weakened by the continual loss of their strongest youngsters, while the Turks maintained military dominance with a near-inexhaustible source of recruits.

[36] Dan II, Vladislav's father and head of the Dăneşti clan, had served as Prince of Wallachia with an amazing five interruptions, losing and retaking the throne by the Ottoman-backed Radu II, between 1420 and 1431. Relations between Vlad II Dracul and the Dăneşti clan had devolved into a full-on feud in the ensuing years, so Vladislav II was more than happy to be complicit in Dracul's ouster.

[37] Boyars were an affluent class of people, perhaps the first upper-middle class-cum-aristocracy that existed in that part of Europe. The boyars often owned vast amounts of land, which they continually enlarged through purchases, calculated marriages, and even through "donations" to princes. Boyars could achieve various hierarchical political titles through service to their prince, military distinction or other merit. With these assets and political power, they diversified by developing incredibly lucrative trade arrangements in their regions, empowering them further. Though the prince was recognized as the supreme commander of the kingdom, where exactly the *real* power resided sometimes got muddy with the entrenched influence wielded by the boyars, whose power predated the formation of the principality. Moreover, as you've no doubt already started to ascertain, princes were a dime a dozen. For example, the average reign for a prince from 1418

loyal to the Dăneşti clan staged a revolt and attacked from the inside.

Mircea was blinded then buried alive. Dracul managed to escape and got almost as far as the settlement later known as Bucharest before the Dăneşti clan caught up with him. They hauled him up to the village of Bălteni in Moldavia for some reason—possibly to elude a rescue attempt by Dracul's remaining allies, but who knows—and then killed him. Dracul's body was carried back to Târgovişte by followers and buried in a nearby monastery, presumably in an unmarked grave. His tomb has still not been found, but a small chapel remains on the spot where Dracul was killed in Bălteni.

When Dracula, then 17, heard about the death of his father and the torturing and burying alive of his brother, whom he still loved and admired, his simmering anger must have gone supernova. With the support of a Turkish cavalry[38],

---

until Dracula's second sitting on the throne (1456-1462) was barely over two years, whereas the boyars' families' power went back for generations. Where they came from and how they achieved this status is under debate. They may have evolved from free landowners, wealthy village leaders, descendants of an old military caste or some combination of these. What's known is they eventually reached a stage of considerable authority sometime before Vlad II's rule. Like today's upper-middle class, some boyars were upstanding, contributing members of society, while others were greedy, power-hungry upstarts who, as conniving, unified factions, had the impetus and resources necessary to dispense with uncooperative princes. Suffice to say, these folks clashed with the Dracul clan *a lot*.

[38] For the moment, despite longstanding tension, Dracula was still considered a friend of Sultan Murad II, so persuading the Sultan to loan out Turkish troops was probably a straightforward matter. It was in the Sultan's best interest to support Vlad's usurping the Wallachian throne,

Vlad Dracula charged into Târgovişte and led a successful coup against the absent Vladislav[39] and took the throne for the first of three sittings in 1448.

Dracula's first reign lasted barely two months before Vladislav returned with Hungarian reinforcements to chase Dracula back to Murad's protection in Ottoman territory.

Vlad later took a calculated risk and fled the protection of the Ottomans and headed for Moldavia, an in-your-face move that presumably marked the beginnings of Dracula's falling out with the Sultan. In Moldavia, Vlad took up residence with his uncle Bogdan II, Prince of Moldavia and, showing impressive patience, spent two years completing his education and forming what would be a crucial bond with his cousin Stephen, who would later become Stephen the Great, ruler of Moldavia for an extraordinary 47 years[40].

---

presumably thereby locking down a long-term ally in a key seat of power on the doorstep of Christian Europe.

[39] Vladislav was in Serbia with John Hunyadi, getting their asses kicked and later fleeing for their lives after a failed attempt to push the Ottomans out of Kosovo.

[40] Forty-seven years in power would be impressive even now, but back in the days of near constant war and turmoil it was downright god-like. Stephen's military battle record was incredible, reportedly losing only 2 out of 50 battles (other sources say 44 victories out of 48 battles) and as a civil ruler he was the next thing to a saint. Indeed, he was named "Athleta Christi" (the Champion of Christ) by Pope Sixtus IV and he was finally canonized by the Romanian Orthodox Church in 1992. After each of his alleged 48 victories, he raised a church or monastery, including some of Romania's famous Painted Churches, noteworthy for having exterior frescoes that have remained remarkably intact, despite being exposed to the elements for centuries. Alas, Stephen's legend could not hold off the Ottomans, who finally secured Moldavia after his death in

Bogdan's murder in 1451 by his brother Petru Aaron forced Dracula and Stephen to flee to Transylvania[41] and into a different kind of trouble when word of Dracula's presence reached the severely politically weakened[42] yet still powerful John Hunyadi.

To review: Hunyadi believed Dracula was in cahoots with the Ottomans and Dracula knew Hunyadi was the architect behind the murders of his father and brother. Though a suicidal rampage to kill Hunyadi must have been awfully tempting, Dracula lay low with Stephen, slinking around Transylvania from Sighişoara to Braşov to Sibiu[43], just ahead of authorities and the assassins Hunyadi sent to arrest or kill Vlad, whichever was most convenient.

Once again, Hunyadi's compulsive thirst for power and pathological character defects eventually eroded relations with his pal Vladislav[44]. Part of their growing rivalry was that Vladislav, like Dracul and Mircea before him, could see no other option but to maintain allegiances with both Hungary *and* the Ottomans, lest Wallachia become embroiled in fighting on two fronts or simply

---

1504.

[41] Via the Borgo Pass!

[42] Hunyadi's two rather extravagant defeats at Varna and Kosovo had resulted in many of his titles being stripped, including Governor of Transylvania, and a complete loss of trust by Hungary.

[43] Dracula had managed to stay in touch with a few friendly boyars in Transylvania and relied on them for refuge.

[44] For reasons lost to time, Hunyadi grabbed the duchies of Făgăraş and Amlaş, both firmly Wallachian territory, which Vladislav rightfully believed were his to rule.

become the smoking, apocalyptic battleground for ongoing border skirmishes between the two empires.

During this time, Dracula's former classmate, Mehmed II, became sultan[45] and Vladislav affably recognized the occasion by sending a delegation to wish him well. This act, and Mehmed's now well-known intention to finally take Constantinople and presumably next go crashing into Christian Europe with this new might, pushed Hungary and Hunyadi into full alarm. And thus, the unthinkable alliance between Hunyadi and Dracula began.

In Hunyadi's eyes, Vlad had two critical things he needed: First, Dracula could bounce the now petulant Vladislav out of Wallachia and, more importantly, Dracula was intimately, pricelessly familiar with not only the tactics of the Ottoman army, but also with Mehmed's own mind. Though Dracula's ears were undoubtedly still smoldering over Hunyadi's role in the murders of his father and brother, there was the long game of princely ambition to take into account. Unbelievably, Dracula was able to quell his emotions and team up with Hunyadi.

Part of this agreement inducted Dracula as a member of Hunyadi's court and furnished him with a residence in Sibiu, much to the chagrin and anxiety of the local Saxons who had been a pain in the asses of Wallachian princes for decades. The two went on a bit of a PR campaign, even traveling together to Buda for the coronation of the new

---

[45] Sultan Murad died of a stroke in February 1451 at age 47.

Hungarian King Ladsilas Posthumus for a very public coming-out of their alliance. Dracula was soon formally put in command of Transylvania's defense against the Turks.

While all this PR spin was going on in Hungary, the situation was getting dire in Constantinople. The Turks were closing in, only paltry help had arrived from the West, and John Hunyadi, whom the Byzantines believed to be their last hope, had despairingly retreated to Transylvania to focus his diminished forces on defending the region. Young Emperor Constantine XI had all but lost the support of Constantinople's citizens. After topping out at a million, the city's population had fled en masse, until only 50,000-60,000 remained, many of whom were superstitious and militarily feeble clerics who had become convinced through a series of "signs" that they were doomed, so there was no point resisting the Ottomans anyway.

Mehmed's forces took the city on May 29, 1453, in one of history's most remarkable victories (or losses, depending on your perspective), which included Constantine's heroic death as he fought among the foot soldiers. News of the murdering, looting, and enslavement of the city rippled across Europe. Official mourning occurred in France, England, and even Moscow. Newly crowned Holy Roman Emperor Frederick III showed token public concern, but he was preoccupied with firming up power and dealing with much closer rivals in Europe and did nothing in response.

Vladislav, though still tight with Mehmed, must have nonetheless lost all bowel control upon hearing the news of the atrocities in Constantinople and wasted no time in making groveling public overtures, reinforcing his allegiance to the Ottomans. A hysterical bishop who had scrambled away from the carnage in Constantinople brought news that Mehmed was planning to swarm up to Serbia with up to 90,000 troops and the support of some 60 ships on the Danube. They would then take the strategic and imposing fortress at Belgrade[46], circle back, stomp Sibiu, and continue on their merry way to pound on Hungary and the Holy Roman Empire. With Vladislav nuzzling the Ottomans' crotches, thereby making Wallachia a kind of military expressway to Transylvania's destruction, the mood in Sibiu was full-on panic.

Hunyadi and Dracula set to work raising funds, hiring mercenaries and arming their forces to defend Transylvania. Hunyadi took the bulk of these troops to the vital fortress at Belgrade and succeeded in defeating the overwhelming Ottoman force, a victory that had the added bonus of wounding Mehmed. Celebrations were brief, as Hunyadi became one of the early victims of the resurging plague and soon died.

---

[46] This incredible, massive fortress was such a powerful stronghold in the 15th century that not only does it still stand today, but it looks like it could still withstand a modern frontal assault. No wonder everyone and his half-brother coveted it.

Vlad's simultaneous mission was to race to Târgovişte, splitting the Ottomans' focus away from Belgrade, and finally face Vladislav in battle. In what must have been the mother of all cathartic moments, Dracula killed Vladislav in hand-to-hand combat, avenging his father and brother. The now 25-year-old Dracula was in full command of Wallachia by August 1456 and immediately got to work helping install his cousin Stephen on the throne in Moldavia, usurping Petru Aaron, Stephen's father's murderer and Ottoman patsy, the following year.

If it hadn't already become obvious, these last two actions convinced whatever allies Dracula had left in Ottoman circles that he was without a doubt no longer their guy, thus triggering escalating hostilities. But before any of that could happen, Dracula had some work to do.

Eyes alive and veritably bugging out with fury, Vlad returned to Târgovişte to consolidate his power, develop and strengthen Wallachia's defenses, and, of course, exact revenge on the hateful boyars who had been involved with burying his brother Mircea alive.

# Târgoviște – The Prince Is in the House

Târgoviște[47], located on the right bank of the Ialomița River, has faded significantly from its heyday as Wallachia's ruling center[48], but it still soldiers nobly, if unassumingly, on as the seat of Dâmbovița County. With a population of 73,964[49], it takes considerable imagination to picture how Târgoviște was once one of the most important cities in Wallachia.

Based on the memoirs of Crusaders and off-the-beaten-medieval-Europe travelers, it's believed that Târgoviște's Princely Court (*"Curtea Domnească"*) began to take shape in the late 14th century, including early fortifications. It was definitely functioning as some kind of fort during the reign of Dracula's granddad, Mircea the Elder (ruled 1386 – 1418), who designated the city as Wallachia's capital by the early 15th century. At the time, Târgoviște was the only town in Wallachia with Transylvanian-style organization, including an entrenched population of those pesky Saxons who tormented, and then were tormented by, Dracula.

Having been the capital of Wallachia since his grandfather's rule, by the time Dracula eased his taut buttocks onto the throne, Târgoviște had developed into a sprawling center of politics and culture and was the social center of the principality. Based on surviving

---

[47] An older spelling is "Tîrgoviște."
[48] Which now, of course, is Bucharest.
[49] Per 2011 census, Romania's 26th-largest city.

correspondence, most of Dracula's testily worded decrees originated from here. It was also, naturally, where Dracula staged some of his most notorious bloodbaths against locals and invaders alike.

The Saxons and Romanians, per usual, mostly stuck to their respective parts of town, with the Saxons and boyars occupying stylish Byzantine houses clustered snugly around the fledgling stronghold, which they dashed into like a medieval Green Zone whenever arrows started flying. Though much of the wealth was predictably rooted in the Saxon part of town, both populations were pretty well off, judging by archeological finds of several large Romanian dwellings complete with cellars and tile stoves, a luxury rarely found east of Central Europe at the time. This wealth was mostly based on Târgovişte's position as a major trade hub in the 15th and 16th centuries, doing much of its business with Poland, Braşov and Sibiu. Trade here became so lucrative that even Greek merchants started horning in on the trade action after 1500.

Târgovişte's becoming the capital of Wallachia and most desirable place to live was no fluke. The city's position and easily accessible resources were a logistical Yahtzee. Târgovişte is strategically located in an indentation of the Carpathian Mountains' foothills, where inhabitants could make a relatively quick retreat and hide out during particularly bad invasions. This indentation is surrounded to the east, west and north by rapidly rising slopes, allowing the capital to concentrate its defenses on the southern flank.

The region also boasts abundant wine production, and fish, even sport fishing for the one-percenters, were plentiful in the city's network of lakes.

Saxon dominance in Târgovişte started to decline only in the 16th century, miraculously enduring through the era when being a greedy, conniving Saxon dog in Wallachia imperiled the security of one's head atop one's body. As the economy faded, so did the Saxons who decamped to more lucrative cities in Transylvania. Those who remained assimilated into the local Romanian population, which grew to be the ethnic majority in the 16th century.

Being a prosperous city and on-again, off-again capital of Wallachia predictably invited attacks and invasion. The Turks, naturally, started things off in 1395 with a siege led by Bayezid I, during which the city was set alight.

Though not all hostility in Târgovişte came from outside forces. With the average half-life of princes in the era, and the sometimes dramatic, caught-with-your-pants-down manner in which power was transferred, it wasn't uncommon for violence to originate from inside the city, including perhaps the most famous house-cleaning incident in the history of Târgovişte, perpetrated by our friend Vlad Dracula. Later, Dracula famously repulsed (more like scared off, if we're splitting hairs) the attempted Ottoman invasion of 1462. More on that in a minute.

The Turks easily overran the Princely Court after Dracula's death in 1476 and held it through innumerable attacks until 1597 when the Hajduks (freedom fighters) of

Mihai Viteazul (Michael the Brave) and Serbia's Starina Novak joined forces to completely remove, at least for a time, the Ottoman Empire from Târgovişte.

After trading the title of capital of Wallachia with Bucharest for two centuries, Bucharest finally became the permanent capital under Constantin Brâncoveanu (1688-1714). As a result, Târgovişte's population slowly declined along with its economic strength.

------------------------------------------------

Both Vlad Dracul and Vlad Dracula made significant updates to the Princely Court complex during their time in power. Vlad Dracul added a discouraging 60-foot moat outside the already formidable perimeter wall. And I mean *discouraging*. One can assume the moat served as drainage for a fair portion of the Princely Court's gutter and sewage runoff and inland moat water recirculation was probably minimal to nonexistent. Also, swimming lessons weren't usually part of the peasant soldier boot camp regimen of the era, so coaxing one's dog-paddling soldiers to march into a stagnant, fetid and unforgiving deathtrap, while dodging arrow fire no less, can't have been an easy task.

After Dracula returned for his second, more substantial sitting on the throne in 1456, anticipating the white-hot Ottoman fury he'd soon be provoking, he added yet another massive wall outside the moat for good measure. He also built the huge (for the time) 73-foot Sunset Tower (aka "*Turnul Chindia*"), providing gravity-assisted defensive capabilities and unrestricted views of the Court's surroundings. Inside these deterrents was the final barrier: the enormous palace itself, with walls as thick as five feet, vast cellars for storing supplies during long sieges, and, it's believed, torture chambers that Dracula used liberally.

Once Dracula's ambitious Sunset Tower was complete, the Princely Court's advanced defenses were a layer cake of escalating certain death. Anyone trying to storm the palace would have to struggle over the outer wall, wade/swim/thrash across the 60-foot moat without swallowing too much poop water, and then scale the inner wall, all the while taking fire from archers on the walls and roof of the palace. Anyone who miraculously made it over these barriers alive was then stuck out in the open between the inner wall and the palace walls, under a hail of point-blank arrow fire, rocks and other skull-crunching items hurled from the watchtower and rooftops. With such well-tended fortifications, it's no wonder that substantial portions of the complex are still standing today[50].

--------------------------

During his second term as prince, the six highly prolific years between 1456 and 1462, Dracula cemented his legacies as Ottoman scourge, national hero, and extravagant, almost unbelievable sadist. He was like the Jack Bauer of Wallachia: patriotic almost to a fault, steadfast in defending the region from external enemies and internal provocateurs,

---

[50] Also, it seems to me the TV show *American Ninja Warrior* owes Dracula's descendents huge royalties.

misunderstood by co-workers, and always ready to face-punch anyone who got in his way.

According to a physical description recorded years later in his early 30s, the portrayal of vampire Count Dracula's frightening appearance didn't take much artistic license from the face of the perma-fuming Prince. According to the chronicler, Vlad had a "cold and terrible appearance," with a beak nose, large nostrils, high cheekbones, and an emaciated face. He was short, but stout, broad-shouldered and apparently quite strong. His large, deep-set, green eyes were penetrating and probably more than a little unsettling—a look his freaky-long eyelashes and generous eyebrows did nothing to soften. Like his shoulder-length hair, Vlad's luxuriant moustache curled at the ends, a look he cultivated counter to the royal style of the time to let moustaches droop down[51].

This written account mostly agrees with the few authentic surviving portraits of Vlad. In any case, one gets the sense that people around him respected his intelligence and intimidating persona, but also feared his virtually glowing-hot aura of cruelty.

While Prince of Wallachia, Dracula's greatest enduring legacy revolved around his enthusiasm for justice via terror and employing inhumanely creative capital-punishment methods, ranging from decapitation to boiling

---

[51] That little is held back in relating Dracula's unflattering features suggests that the author of this description may not have been entirely taken by Vlad's charms.

and burying alive. His posthumous moniker "Ţepeş" (The Impaler) was designated due to his favorite form of pre-death torture: a dull, greased wooden stake was judiciously driven through the victim's anus, emerging from the body just below the shoulder blades without piercing any vital organs, causing up to 48 hours of unimaginable agony before death. When short on time, Dracula would resort to more practical impaling methods through the chest, abdomen and heart.

Impaling was done in public. Târgovişte's town squares had permanent stakes driven into the ground so that an impaling could be performed with minimal preparation. Dracula frequently attended these impalings, as one does, and when he was feeling extra theatrical he would have the victim held in place above the tip of a stake, strap each of his or her legs to horses and then have the beasts trot away in opposite directions.

Even in an era when human life was unbelievably cheap, one in which witnessing death was a regular occurrence for most people, these gory, slow-motion spectacles must have been appalling.

A famous wood etching shows Ţepeş enjoying a full meal while watching boyars writhe on stakes in front of him. It's theorized that this image was key to inspiring Stoker to remake Dracula into a monster.

Not one to disregard creativity or variety, Vlad made lavish use of many other forms of torture and killing of the time, including cutting off facial features, limbs, and sexual organs, blinding, boiling, burning, hanging, strangling, crucifying, skinning alive, and burying alive. Conniving boyars and Saxon merchants were most often the target of his cruelty. Even their wives and children weren't spared grotesque and prolonged deaths[52], including an oft-told tale of a merciless mother-child combo killing method that involved a woman being staked in both breasts and her children being run through on the protruding stakes, affixing them to her chest.

At times, the stakes and tree limbs surrounding Dracula's palace were teeming with impaled and hanging corpses, which people were strictly forbidden to take down. The stink of rotting bodies must have been overpowering at the height of summer.

While Dracula had a hair-trigger for impaling those who had the power to threaten his rule, or even mildly irritate him, his converse compassion for those in the peasant classes is sometimes compared to (an extremely violent) Robin Hood. In truth, his reputation for favoring the poor was largely a pragmatic strategy. The peasant class made up some 90 percent of Wallachia's citizens at the time and Dracula needed them on his side, both for joining him in battle and for the sheer manpower needed to sustain Wallachia's agricultural output, which Dracula believed was the region's primary asset. Those fields weren't going to tend

---

[52] The logic of the day was if one didn't wipe out his enemy's entire family, some relative or descendent would someday muster a revenge campaign—and who needs that unnecessary distraction?

themselves. That said, he certainly didn't hesitate to gut-stab any peasant who gave him lip or even appeared to be a little bit lazy.

In all fairness to Vlad, this caliber of unchained violence and hideous punishments wasn't unusual in medieval Europe. Contemporaries in France and Italy made a habit of murdering political opponents and slaughtering their families for good measure. The Saxons in Braşov routinely staked convicted murders and, by comparison, impaling was really no worse than Roman crucifixions or the techniques used in the Spanish Inquisition. Though he's sometimes erroneously credited for having invented the practice of impaling enemies, Vlad may have first witnessed staking in Transylvania as a child and he almost definitely saw other instances during his time in the Turkish court[53], which of course came back to haunt the Turks when he was terrorizing them in battle. That said, there's no denying that Dracula took the practice to previously unimaginable scales of application.

It should also be noted that Vlad's first cousin, the aforementioned Stephen the Great, much celebrated Prince of Moldavia, is said to have "impaled by the navel, diagonally, one on top of each other" 2,300 Turkish prisoners in 1473. And they *sainted* that guy!

---

[53] If not at that time, then he certainly heard about the Ottomans staking numerous prisoners as an intimidation tactic while attacking Constantinople in 1453.

That said, it's difficult to argue that Dracula wasn't just unhinged, but also unpredictable. Near the end of his reign, even his allies began to abandon him—partly for his frequent bouts of senseless violence and killing, but also because there was no telling when or for what trivial reason Dracula might turn on them.

Like his father, Dracula would spend much of his time in power harassing or being harassed by one force or another. Though it paled in comparison to the Ottoman hoarde he would eventually face, Dracula in fact commanded a relatively large, organized force. Wallachia's army brought together a tenacious and driven combination of free peasants and boyars who were downright enthusiastic about going to war to defend their territory.

In the beginning, the Ottomans would disastrously underestimate the scale of the campaign necessary to beat the Wallachians. After easily rolling over the disorganized and feeble feudal armies in Bulgaria and Serbia, the Ottoman swagger wasn't prepared for Dracula's well-trained, highly motivated band. But I've gotten ahead of myself.

------------------------------

With his newly fortified stronghold in place at Târgoviște, Vlad could finally get down to dishing out some long overdue retribution. The sniveling boyars responsible for the horrible deaths of his father and brother already had stakes with their names on them, obviously. But Dracula was also intent on thinning the herd of boyars, those leading citizens and their families who had been working diligently for decades to destabilize the principality to their benefit and unseat a quick succession of princes who dared defy them.

As an apparently plausible gesture of goodwill, Dracula invited the boyars and their families to an Easter feast in the Princely Court's new great hall. For stupefying reasons about which one can only speculate, the boyars accepted this invitation, arriving en masse, families in tow, suspecting nothing and ready to get their drink on. One presumes Vlad stood up after dinner, delivered a sinister, butthole-constricting monologue on the topics of treachery and unconventional uses for human orifices, savored the moment for theatrical effect as his guests started nervously inching towards the exits, then had them lined up and impaled—some 500 of them. Thus began Dracula's legend for elaborate, unforgiving cruelty.

The boyars killed on the spot[54] were the lucky ones. Not so lucky were those who were marched to the Wallachia-

---

[54] Wiping out about 90 percent of his upper and ruling class in one fell swoop was a debilitating reduction of governing power that even Dracula knew wasn't going to work out. He filled these roles with a variety of people, including common citizens, peasants, and gypsies as well as foreigners including Turks, Serbs, Tartars and even Hungarians, many of whom happily received the vacated lands and possessions of the recently dispatched boyars. He did the same when filling high positions such as governors and diplomats. By doing this, he created an instant administrative body and fiercely loyal security force that was greatly appreciative of his generosity and therefore highly invested in his continued reign. This carefully engineered autocratic system, with tantalizing perks given to those who remained loyal, also made raising a committed, unyielding army fairly straightforward. Thus, he had ingeniously consolidated power and had the muscle to enforce it in two

Transylvania border, where they were put to work building Phase Two of Vlad's defensive plans, Poenari Castle, which we'll learn about later.

Dracula's extreme intolerance for crime quickly became legend in Wallachia and lands beyond. Even after the mass slaughter of the boyars in 1456, an event one would think would have gone a long way toward discouraging misdeeds, crime in Wallachia was still rife. Dracula didn't hesitate to make an example of a few poor souls and soon crime all but ceased for the remainder of his reign.

One early incident in Târgovişte set the tone for his ruthless attitude toward crime. After a local had stolen 160 ducats from a merchant passing through town, Dracula declared that *all* of Târgovişte was responsible for finding the culprit; if the citizens failed, he vowed to raze the entire city. The thief was located and handed over with all due haste.

In another incident, when a high-ranking gypsy was convicted of theft, in what may have been a last-ditch attempt to avoid execution, he declared to Dracula that impaling and burning alive were against the sacred laws of his people. So, Dracula had him boiled alive in a gigantic cauldron[55]. Still unconvinced that true punishment had been served, Dracula then forced the gypsy's tribe to eat the cooked flesh[56].

---

relatively quick moves.

[55] I love that they had human-sized cauldrons sitting around for just such occasions in the 15th century.

Another famous anecdote involved a golden cup that Vlad placed at a popular, but secluded fountain in town—a tantalizing snatch-and-run opportunity. But by this stage, tales of Dracula's enthusiastic staking aptitude had already circulated to Italy and beyond. As such, locals and travelers alike were too petrified to touch the cup. It sat on the fountain unmolested until, one assumes, convincing evidence had been received that Dracula was out of the picture.

Admirable as his passion was for ridding his realm of crime, Dracula's sanctimonious street cleaning gets a little muddy when it comes to his treatment of Wallachia's sick, disabled and, in particular, beggars. He equated begging to slow-motion, never-ending thievery and, as we know, Dracula did not suffer thieves in his 'hood. In one oft-repeated infamous story, Dracula lured the beggars of the region to a local house, promising them new clothes and a lavish feast. Well, of course every beggar for miles showed up. While they ate and drank themselves blind, Dracula excused himself, bolted the door from the outside and set the house on fire[57].

------------------------------

[56] Allegedly!

[57] And these acts of brutality are nothing compared to the folklore written by distant writers hungry to make a buck or just fostering the rampant Dracula smearing that ensued after his death. The Germans and Russians were particularly creative in this regard, with tales so gruesome I have elected to not include them here.

Today the Princely Court is little Târgoviște's primary tourist attraction, and the 15th-century Sunset Tower is considered the symbol of the city. The Sunset Tower was, of course, first used for military and defensive purposes. It later served as a guard point, fire-spotting station and for treasury storage. The Tower, which grew to a height of 89 feet during a 19th-century restoration project, now serves as a museum where visitors can view a collection of Dracula's documents, weapons, and other personal objects. It's also possible to climb the Tower where one is rewarded with a bird's-eye view photo opportunity of the entire Princely Court complex. There's also a nice long view of Târgoviște itself, sprawling mainly to the south and east, including innumerable church bell towers, red-tiled roofs of squat houses and, farther out, the familiar Soviet, unsightly, gray cement apartment blocks in the outer rings of the city.

The condition of the site's surviving ruins are quite impressive for being a much-attacked and interfered with 15th-century complex. Some ruins are barely knee-high and don't give much more than an impression of the structure's foundation. Others are quite substantial, including the main palace where one can easily discern cellars, aqueducts, windows, doorways, tunnels and sections of wall exceeding 30 feet high. Apart from the arresting palace ruins, the complex also has the remains of two princes' houses, a ruined church and two intact churches dating from the 16th century, one of which is a museum with 18th-century frescoes.

In the park just north of the Princely Court ruins is a worthwhile photo op: a chorus line of busts of Wallachia's princes, except for Vlad who is suitably honored with a much larger statue in the park's center. He's depicted looking wild-eyed and brandishing a sword, which, one imagines, spent more time exploring internal organs than a swallowed piece of gum.

Finally, on the outskirts of the city, there are surviving ruins of a 14th-century Franciscan church that was, of course, in use during Dracula's time, though it's unknown if Vlad himself ever worshipped there.

------------------------------------------

When I rolled into Târgoviște for the first time in March 2006, I must admit, I was not at my best. Winter was still hanging tenaciously, diabolically over the region. Snow coated the ground, both making it slippery and camouflaging the remarkable potholes on Romania's famously busted, pre-European Union-funded roads.

The size of Târgoviște and its limited offerings makes it a three-hour guidebook research stop at best, so I never spent the night in the city or even explored it too thoroughly apart from its tourist attractions. Outside of the Princely Court, all that was on my fact-checking plate was a handful of minor, tightly clustered museums, a couple of nearby budget hotels (the only kind in Târgoviște), a few places to get subsistence meals, the train station, and other quick odds and ends. When you research lesser cities like this, efficiency is key so the bulk of your resources can be applied to higher-profile sites and destinations.

Which is why, on that god-awful day in 2006, I was scream-cursing 15 minutes after driving into the city and still no closer to locating the goddamn Princely Court. Like much of Romania, the notion of conspicuously posted street names and basic signage to help out-of-towners had not yet occurred to Târgovişte's civic leaders[58]. Despite its small size, and having just one rather important tourist sight, I had become disproportionally, absurdly lost while meandering through the historic center's confounding streets, which, I theorized at the top of my lungs, had been plotted by a blindfolded, three-legged donkey. Several costly ice ages later, I finally zigzagged up to the complex on the northern edge of town.

Even in summer Târgovişte isn't exactly overwhelmed with tourists, but at the tail end of an especially nasty winter I was pretty sure I was the only foreign tourist for 100 kilometers in any direction. Even Romanians were thin on the ground at tourist sites that time of year. Throughout my tour of Wallachia, I'd had most tourist sights pretty much to myself and the same was true of the Princely Court.

When you visit third-tier tourist sites during Romania's slow season, you often find the ticket windows at

---

[58] Even Bucharest famously didn't have signs pointing the way to important items like the main train station or the airport until fairly recently. Though, in their defense, signs pointing the way to every McDonald's in town were thorough and exhaustive.

the gates of said sites abandoned, which now was once again the case. Seeing no one around who seemed likely to take my money in exchange for a ticket, I just wandered through the open gate.

One of the many exhausting aspects of researching a guidebook in a place like Romania is how much things change in only two years. In Tuscany? Nothing changes. Hotels, restaurants, and historic sites, obviously, are operated seamlessly for decades and even centuries, usually by successive generations of the same family. Thus, researching a Tuscany guidebook is mainly an exercise in updating prices and ever-fluctuating museum hours. In Romania, however, in two years' time places sometimes become straight-up unrecognizable. Hotels are abandoned, formerly good restaurants become strip clubs, internet cafes come and go in a span of six weeks, and even paragraphs about sites that have stood for centuries need editing.

I arrived at the Princely Court disappointed to find it undergoing heavy restoration work, though, despite being the middle of the afternoon on a weekday, there wasn't a worker in sight. Many sections of the site were covered in tarps and protective glass, and the main attraction, the Sunset Tower, was closed. I tried the door of the tower anyway in case it was unlocked—you'd be surprised how often this is the case in Romania—but alas it was secured.

I let out a mushroom-cloud caliber sigh for something like the 25th time that day and did my best to scout the site, checking whatever facts I could. The current configuration of the complex is about one generous city block in area, with a much more modest perimeter wall than when it was at its formidable, Ottoman-repulsing peak. I crunched around in the snow, circling and crisscrossing the complex trying to discern features described in the text of the guidebook's previous edition.

For whatever reason details were thin in the previous edition, so I decided to make a comprehensive reconnaissance of the site, taking speculative notes on what I was seeing, which I was able to cross-check with information in a helpful brochure that I had picked up in one of the lesser museums in town. I later learned the thin information in the guidebook was due to the word-count limit of that section and I too was eventually forced to abandon my hard-won, diligently researched and written additions to the site description, all just to stay under the word-count limit. One of the many hair-yanking, whimpering lessons I learned during that first guidebook project was that one shouldn't start writing new content until one knows where they stand on the word count[59].

When I find myself all alone in what is, or at least should be, an extremely important historic site, I tend to want to hang around enjoying my sole, unfettered access and poking my nose into areas where visitors aren't normally allowed to poke. I indulged in this for quite some time at the Princely Court, but the sun was getting low and I

---

[59] Pro tip!

had a room reserved 80 kilometers away in Piteşti. The combination of the nasty roads and the pathetic headlights on the Dacia meant driving too long after sunset wasn't prudent. I walked back through the still unattended entrance/exit, turned around, tried to imagine Vlad and his team hard at work introducing stakes into Turkish assholes, and then walked quickly toward my next objective.

-------------------------------------

Târgovişte is famously associated with another brutal ruler. It was here on December 25th, 1989, in a military barracks just north of the train station, that hated dictator Nicolae Ceauşescu and his royal pill of a wife Elena were croaked by their own military in a hail of bullets, bringing the Romanian Revolution to a swift and decisive end.

Though revolts by Romania's pissed-off and desperate population had already begun in other cities (and were swiftly crushed), it was in the western city of Timişoara that the 1989 Romanian Revolution finally got its footing. That Ceauşescu had never been popular in Timişoara, even at the height of his power, was probably a factor leading the inhabitants to mount the first legitimate resistance. Even at peak ego-bulge, Ceauşescu never felt safe there. During his 25 years in power, Ceauşescu paid only a few brief visits to the city, always with complex surreptitious travel and sleeping arrangements to pacify his assassination concerns[60].

---

[60] For quite some time, Timişoara had a rather morbid, low-key

In December 1989, truculent Timişoara was primed for rebellion for pretty much any reason, and the always overconfident, brutal Securitate gave them one.

A young, local Hungarian pastor by the name of László Tőkés had long been one of Ceauşescu's most outspoken critics. Unaccustomed at this stage to anyone having the balls to disparage him publicly, Ceauşescu, after what was probably less than a moment of consideration, ordered his people to have Tőkés taken to the Hungarian border and catapulted over the fence. (Or so I have imagined it.)

When Tőkés' parishioners heard about his imminent deportation, they formed a human chain around his block on December 15th. This effort to protect him from arrest mushroomed and lost all focus. Many of the protesters who spontaneously joined the initial rally mistakenly thought they were demonstrating for religious freedom, not for the defense of Tőkés. Like I said, the Timişoarans were ready to rebel against pretty much anything.

Within days, the protest had turned into a full-scale, anti-Communist revolt. A breathtakingly overconfident Ceauşescu actually left Romania during this time for a visit

---

attraction: Villa International Hotel had an apartment-style suite, which was available to any guest who elected to pay the extortionate price; the Ceauşescus had once slept there for two nights. The room was preserved exactly as it was when the Ceauşescus had stayed in it (as was the entire hotel, by the looks of it when I visited), including several personal effects the couple had left behind. Sometime between my first and second visits to Timişoara, the hotel went through a comprehensive renovation and the Ceauşescus' room was finally gutted.

to Iran, leaving various subordinates and his wife Elena—by all accounts even dumber and crueler than Nicolae—to deal with the escalating protests.

Not quite understanding the scope of the deteriorating predicament, Party officials brought in club-wielding factory workers to attack the protesters, but instead the workers joined the protesters. Demonstrations were centered in what was then known as Piaţa Operei (Opera Square), today known as Piaţa Victoriei (Victory Square!). The crowds chanted anti-government slogans and sung an old, banned Romanian anthem called "Wake up, Romanians!"

On December 17th, a combined force of military, police and Securitate agents fired indiscriminately into the crowd.

By the time Ceauşescu returned to Romania from Iran, the situation was critical. The demonstration had swelled to some 100,000 people and overran the military, commandeering some of the tanks that had previously fired on demonstrators. By December 19th—whether out of fear or having just decided "fuck this"—the military switched sides. Roughly 115 people had been killed.

Despite a state media blackout, word of the courageous happenings in Timişoara had reached the rest of the country and Bucharest via Western radio stations like Voice of America and Radio Free Europe.

On December 21st Ceauşescu addressed a crowd in Bucharest from the balcony of the Central Committee building at a staged "rally," designed to make it appear that he still had the support of the masses, blaming the Timişoara protests on "fascist agitators." Unaware that pretty much everyone knew what was really happening in Timişoara, he lost his audience in mere minutes. Booing and shouting began, intensifying rapidly. People yelled "murderer" and chanted "Ti-mi-şoa-ra."

Looking both confused and a little rattled (megalomaniacs often have difficulty processing the concept of mass revolt), he attempted to win the crowd back by promising to raise the minimum wage. Unyielding, the crowd resumed the verbal abuse. Television coverage of the rally was abruptly cut off and the Ceauşescus disappeared into the Central Committee building where they were forced to spend the night.

Meanwhile, the military was sent in to deal with the defiant protesters. When the crowds retreated to the main boulevard connecting Piaţa Universitatii and Piaţa Romana, they encountered gunfire and armored cars. The demonstrators started erecting barricades as the military attempted to drive them back with ice-cold water from fire hoses. All of this was happening in full view of Western journalists who had been confined to the adjacent Hotel Inter-Continental.

At 11:00 p.m. the police used a tank to smash through the barricade and began attacking the protesters. It's believed at least 1,033 were killed, though it is impossible to determine a precise number. By the time the sun came up on

December 22, the square had been thoroughly, chillingly cleared of all evidence of the previous night's violence, debris and bodies.

Undeterred, thousands of demonstrators once again filled the streets of Bucharest and protests broke out in cities across Romania. Ceauşescu declared a state of emergency.

At noon, a nervous and fatigued-looking Nicolae once again attempted to address the crowds from the balcony of the Central Committee building, but his fate was sealed before he'd uttered a single syllable. Unbeknownst to Nicolae, news had gotten out that Romania's defense minister had suddenly died. It was eventually ruled a suicide, but the rumor rapidly spreading through the military at the time was that their leader had been murdered. When Ceauşescu promptly took command of the army, the soldiers, believing that the duplicitous dictator was behind the killing of their leader, sided with the protesters *en masse*.

Surrounded by tens of thousands of enraged protesters who were now hurling objects at the balcony, and with any semblance of protection evaporating, the Ceauşescus were forced to retreat inside. Protesters beat down the doors of the now undefended Central Committee building, overpowered what was left of Ceauşescu's guards, and started heading for the balcony. Having fled to the roof, the Ceauşescus, one of their vice presidents, and three bodyguards squeezed into four seats in a waiting helicopter and took off only moments before the mob reached the roof.

The helicopter raced to the presidential suite in the town of Snagov, 40 kilometers (25 miles) north of Bucharest. It was a brief stop. A call to a unit commander to summon soldiers for protection ended with the commander informing them "There has been a revolution... You are on your own... Good luck!"

The Ceauşescus and two Securitate guards jumped back into the helicopter. Ceauşescu's personal pilot, probably unwilling to die in the crossfire for Nicolae's dumb ass, began performing rollercoaster-like climbs and dives to frighten his passengers, saying (lying) this would keep them from being hit by anti-aircraft fire. The ruse worked. An increasingly panicked Nicolae had the pilot land the helicopter.

The Ceauşescus and their guards flagged down a few cars. One driver faked engine trouble to get himself out of the situation. The group was eventually able to convince a no-doubt terrified local to pick them up. For lack of any better ideas, the driver took them to his place of work, an agricultural institute outside good ol' Târgovişte. The institute's director, showing incredible poise, convinced the group to hide in a room. He then locked the door and called the police. The Ceauşescus were apprehended and taken to Târgovişte's military base.

On Christmas Day, with virtually no allies left and plenty of opportunistic rivals waiting to take power (more on that later), Nicolae and Elena were shoved into a make-shift courtroom. In proceedings that lasted barely an hour, they were tried and condemned to death for genocide, embezzlement of state wealth and sabotaging the economy. The entire "trial" was recorded by TV cameras and later broadcast.

Nicolae and Elena protested and verbally abused their prosecutors the entire time, but lost their nerve when they were ordered to be shot immediately by a firing squad consisting of three soldiers—though it's said hundreds volunteered. The Ceaușescus were tied up and thrown against a wall and the enthusiastic soldiers opened fire before the TV camera had time to start recording. When the camera was ready, the soldiers fired again for show, shooting at the bare wall and the dirt where the Ceaușescus' bodies already lay. All of this was later broadcast while the stunned country celebrated Christmas.

In the aftermath, a TV crew was allowed into the Ceaușescus' luxurious apartments and screens across the country lit up with images of food scales made of gold in the kitchen and Elena's rows of diamond-studded shoes.

Though there probably wasn't a soul in Romania who didn't think the Ceaușescus were horrible, vindictive, murderous people who had driven their country to ruin through a dangerous mix of arrogance and stupidity, many express doubt and regret to this day about the manner and swiftness of the trial, particularly those directly involved. Literally no evidence was presented. The chief military judge deliberated for only a few minutes. There wasn't even a passing attempt to demonstrate due process. The chief military judge, Gica Popa, killed himself a decade later, some believe due to inconsolable guilt.

Romania was the only ex-Soviet state to violently unseat their leader. The Ceauşescus final footnote in Romanian history was that they were the last people to be executed in Romania before capital punishment was abolished in January 1990.

Sounds like a classic case of an oppressed population rising up to bounce a hated dictator, right? Not so fast! In the years since, with new details emerging, scholars generally believe that Ceauşescu was probably unknowingly facing an imminent coup d'etat by Communist Party rivals who had grown weary of his ego, bullshit, and incompetence. When the 1989 Revolution heated up, Ceauşescu's scheming usurpers just calmly stepped back and let the people do the job for them, possibly supplying a little quiet, back-channel assistance.

These bystanders promptly took power after Ceauşescu's murder, rebranding their party as the "National Salvation Front" (NSF). In truth, these dipshits weren't much better, kinder or smarter than Ceauşescu, and Romania continued to suffer for years.

-------------------------------------------

Flash to present-day Târgovişte. After decades of limited public access to the military barracks where the Ceauşescus were killed, even a strict photo ban on the property extending as far as the street outside the walls, in 2013 the base was opened as a tourist site, part of the questionably tasteful trail of "Dictator Tourism" that Romania began quietly promoting in 2011[61]. One can step into the courtyard where the Ceauşescus were killed and see the bullet marks from the firing squad still visible on the wall. White outlines painted on the pavement show where their bodies fell.

If you're lucky, you'll get to talk to the museum's director, Ovidiu Carstina, who can sometimes be persuaded to recount stories of the Ceauşescus and their brief detainment and trial in Târgovişte.

---

[61] In March 2016, they finally opened Ceauşecu's 80-room mansion in Bucharest to visitors, which includes a cinema, a pool and an "impressive" dressing room.

# Poenari Castle – Stronghold, sweet stronghold

As we already know, Ţepeş and his forces staked ass and took names right out of the gate as they dealt with the aristocratic, greedy boyars whose shady dealings he directly blamed for Wallachia's strife and corruption. There was also the none-too-trivial matter of their role in the murder of his father and stepbrother, which meant they would probably take a shot at Vlad sooner or later.

While dispensing with several hundred of those responsible for previous offenses at the Easter massacre in Târgovişte, as well as a horde of potential saboteurs for the sake of thoroughness, the ever-practical Dracula had the presence of mind to keep dozens alive for slave labor. And with the impending incursions of uninvited foreign guests from one or more directions looking more likely every day, he had the perfect project for them. Still wearing their Easter duds, Vlad marched this chain gang of dandies to the border of Wallachia and Transylvania in the Carpathian Mountains. At a strategic pass, the prisoners were put to work building Dracula's combination treasury and last-ditch panic room— Poenari Castle.

-----------------------------------------

Even today, getting to Poenari Castle takes a daunting amount of effort. In the 15th century, traveling there must have been like going to Guam in terms of the spine-jangling, ass-flattening hours spent in an uncomfortable, turbulent seat. Assuming moderate zigzagging to negotiate the foothills en route, it must have been at least 100 kilometers (62 miles) on horseback from Vlad's office at Târgovişte to this mountain stronghold. Not exactly a pleasant commute.

Unless one is up for braving rural bus routes, sitting between a soon-to-be-food live chicken and a shepherd who hasn't showered since Christmas, the only sane way to get to Poenari is by car. Though people who feel like they need to suffer in order to "earn" travel fulfillment could conceivably take a train to Curtea de Argeş, about 27 kilometers away, and hitchhike from there. Have fun!

Even in a car, however, the trip can be punishing. Though the roads in Romania have improved immensely since EU funds started rolling in, some of the lesser countryside roads are still rough enough to make parts fall off your car and your head snap around like a boxer's speedball.

Most people approach from Bucharest, in the southeast. The roads from this direction, fortunately, are in great condition. The bad news? They're so well maintained because many of Romania's industrial products from locations across Wallachia roll over these roads on their way to Bucharest and the port in Constanta for sale and export. The stretch from Bucharest to Piteşti is especially pristine, as this is where the Dacia, Romania's national car[62], has

---

[62] Now owned by French car manufacturer Renault.

been manufactured since 1966. As such, this part of Romania is arguably the least scenic, so it's doubly nice these roads allow one to race at top speed for much of the 180-kilometer (112 mile) distance from Bucharest to Poenari.

Once you've rattled up to Poenari and used a tree to pop your Th9 vertebra back into place, there's still the matter of climbing up to that bastard, 860 meters (2,822 feet) above the Argeş River valley. In 1970, Romanian authorities decided to make Poenari a little more tourist-friendly and carved 1,480 steps into the rock of the mountain leading up from the road. Before that, it was likely a knee-skinning, branch-clutching scramble to reach the castle.

You would assume that with the castle's historical significance, and Dracula's status as a hero in Romania, Poenari would be swarming with vacationing Romanians and busloads of day-tripping foreigners. On the contrary, I've visited the site four times now and only once did I have any company at the top. Even the ticket booth has been abandoned three out of four times. Admittedly, most of these visits transpired during mid and low season, but it still struck me as strange, like having Notre Dame all to myself.

I suspect the 1,480 steps are a deal-breaker for many prospective visitors, who can, after all, see more photogenic things just a few hours north in Transylvania without risking cardiac infarction. Even though most of the steps aren't particularly steep, such a climb requires a modest degree of fitness.

While getting to Poenari is still a pain in the everything, even in a comfortable car and with perfect weather, you are rewarded upon arrival with delightful photo opportunities of the ruins and an expansive view from the peak—all without some doofus tourist's recently purchased "Dracula Sucks!" hat sullying the frame.

Construction of the original castle on this site began in the 13th century, under the rule of the upbeat-sounding "Black King." Anyone's residence in a coveted castle like this was notoriously short in medieval times, so the property went through several changes in name and owners over the decades before the castle was abandoned and left in ruins. Seeing its defensive and strategic importance, however, Vlad got to work rebuilding the castle in the 15th century. And by "Vlad," I of course mean his new, miserable work crew who were recently whip-marched in from Târgoviște.

Fearing rebellion, attack and/or assassination by a number of enemies, frenemies and reprobates, Dracula needed Poenari built in a hurry so he'd have a safe retreat where he could sharpen stakes for the eventual retaliation rampage. This urgency is likely why Poenari was erected on the existing stone base, with the remainder built with more efficient brick—something visitors can still appreciate in the ruins.

Though slave labor did perform the bulk of the work, there are signs that master craftsmen also worked on the castle. Since Vlad rightly assumed he might have to repulse waves of enraged adversaries, no expense was spared on the walls, which were nine feet thick in places. A Byzantine method was used to fortify the walls, where two external walls were built in brick with a gap in between. Rubble was then poured in to fill the gap, making it remarkably strong.

Since Poenari was, and still is, in a lively earthquake zone, lime mortar was used to hold the walls together instead of cement, allowing for flexibility when the ground begins to dance. Also, and most ingeniously, the roof of the castle was designed to collect rainwater and feed it into a storage system, so in the event of an especially long siege, the occupants wouldn't die of dehydration. Though any evidence of it is gone, it's believed there was also a well inside the fortress to go along with (and this is pure speculation) a hidden passage that descended deep into the mountain. This passage would have connected with a cave down by the river and possibly allowed Dracula to escape a desperate Ottoman siege in 1462.

Despite the speed and unskilled labor that went into constructing the castle, the completed structure was all but impossible to breach. Almost 600 years later, many of the castle's walls are still standing[63].

Sand, gravel, river stones, bricks and other materials needed to build the castle were readily available in the valley below. Dracula had sent previous orders to the peasants of

---

[63] With some restoration.

the villages below to build brick ovens and lime kilns. When he arrived with his enslaved boyars, they were put to work making bricks and passing them hand-to-hand in a human chain up the hill. It was almost certainly a living hell, with people perishing daily from exhaustion, hunger, and whippings, or simply losing their tired footing on the hill and tumbling down into the valley, coming to a rest in a pile of mangled limbs in the river. Those who somehow survived worked so hard that their clothes literally fell off, leaving them to work naked. Walking today's steps, even without the weight of bricks and stones, the climb will test your glutes and hamstrings and probably leave you walking funny the next day. In short, it's safe to assume people were expiring left and right during construction.

When completed, probably in a matter of months, the castle filled the entire summit, a relatively modest area ranging from 32 to 100 feet wide and 180 feet long from tip to tip. After taking into account the thickness of the walls, which were built to withstand cannon fire, the actual living space inside was pretty spare. There were five towers, of which the remains of two are distinguishable today; they could house anywhere from 20 to 30 soldiers, plus Dracula, his wife, and a number of servants in the event of an extended siege. Outside the walls were servants' quarters[64], stables, outhouses and the like, all of which are gone now.

---

[64] Blatant disregard for the wellbeing of one's servants was, apparently, the norm.

Being an effectively invincible structure perched at the top of a grueling slope allowed Poenari's defenders to lazily pick off anyone crazy enough to storm the castle, merely using arrows or hurling rocks over the side. It also gave Dracula a literal bird's-eye view of the strategic pass between the mountains separating Transylvania and Wallachia.

The castle was used for many years after Vlad's death in 1476, but it was eventually abandoned again in the first half of the 16th century[65] and fell to ruins by the 17th century. In 1888 a landslide caused a substantial part of the structure to collapse and tumble into the valley below. What remains today are mostly head-high ruins.

------------------------------------

For the most part, Romania's tourism instincts and promotional campaigns range from pitiable to comical. If you're curious about how un-fucking-believably hapless Romania's tourism ministry is, search for the music video "Romania – Land of Choice," released in early 2009. Though they've done an admirable job of scrubbing it from the internet, with the help of key Romanian search words, it can probably still be found. Warning: This painfully uninspired, lazily composed, pan flute-heavy disaster cannot be un-watched, no matter how much you wish it could. Several

---

[65] When the Ottomans were in full control of the area, the strategic significance of the fortress was rendered moot.

parody videos exist, too, like the hilariously bitter "The End of Choice," so happy hunting.

Are you back? Good. Now that you've seen an example of the little to nonexistent consideration that goes into Romanian tourism decisions, it will come as no surprise to hear that around 2010 some halfwit official came along and enriched Poenari with cheesy photo op exhibits, including prisoner stocks, a hangman's noose, and two life-sized dolls messily impaled on stakes. And I'm not talking about down on the road by the souvenir stands where that kind of idiocy belongs. No, it's up at the top of the hill, next to the castle entrance, ruining the sightlines for people who actually want to photograph the castle. Bravo, dumbshits.

A less disappointing addition are the signs posted at intervals along the 1,480 steps. Printed in Romanian and English, they detail the history of Poenari for people taking a breather during the climb. These are actually quite helpful, particularly if you have the brains to leave the heavy guidebook in the car before starting your ascent.

The last part of the climb, a moderately steep, but nevertheless dispiriting cement staircase, reliably causes one (me) to release an involuntary, beleaguered sigh, particularly if one (me) fails to pace himself during the first 1,460 steps. Once this hurdle is overcome, there's the immediate reward of the view. The expansive panorama of green, mountainous splendor will, if it hasn't happened already, convert the most jaded soul into a helpless Romania-ophile.

Entering what remains of the castle's doorway, you walk down a narrow passageway, lined by the tallest of the castle's remaining brick walls (roughly 15 feet high) which then opens up into a low-walled, gaping vista of ruins, mountains and sky.

A few very un-Romanian-like safety measures in the form of hand railings and single-cross-bar obstructions have been haphazardly placed around the edges of the ruins to keep idiots from falling to their stupid deaths. These are so easily overcome, and being that there's zero supervision, you might almost feel compelled to inch out on to the edge of the ruins for a good photo, all while standing on a crumbling scrap of 600-year-old brick, with the glorious Făgăraş Mountains as a backdrop.

Walking the length of the castle, the decapitated remains of turrets and a square watchtower are plainly discernable. The watchtower portion, accessed through the lone surviving arched doorway, contains a deep chasm that could have been either the dungeon or the medieval toilet's septic tank. Or, knowing Vlad's capacity for unremitting cruelty, perhaps both.

Despite the generous dimensions described earlier, the thick walls bite into the square footage and make the interior footprint of Poenari feel worryingly snug. Looking at renderings of Poenari in its sturdy, un-collapsed prime, and taking into account the meager shelter provided by the squat turrets and (formerly) three-level watch tower—with the remainder of Poenari left open to the elements—the living conditions inside the castle seem pretty wretched for people twiddling their thumbs while waiting out an enemy attack.

During communist times, privileged Romanians and tourists alike were allowed to sleep in the castle ruins, which, considering the uneven, rocky ground, and the complete lack of shelter and bathroom facilities, seems like something more fitting for prisoners needing that one last push before confessing to murder.

Ultimately, inspecting the surviving walls, speculating about what bits served what purpose, and taking 935 pictures of the view is about all Poenari has to offer. Even allowing for time to space out while studying the view, it's a 45-minute visit, maximum. Then it's back down those effing steps, which are pure hell on the quadriceps after a few minutes. The good news is that the subsequent leg soreness will be nicely distributed among all the muscles, ensuring that *every* move hurts.

A couple of miles south of Poenari is the village of Arefu, whose inhabitants, the Dobrin clan, famously helped Dracula escape Poenari while it was surrounded in 1462 by Turks intent on rearranging Dracula extremities[66]. In thanks, Vlad rewarded them with 16 mountains and 14 sheepfolds' worth of pasturelands, an agreement that amazingly seems to have been honored even during Ceaușescu's mass collectivization of land. Perhaps

---

[66] More on that alarming tale later on.

Ceauşescu thought it better to not risk enraging the ghost of one of Romania's most vindictive leaders.

Arefu is the quintessential Romanian village—with its dirt streets that turn to hopeless mud slicks when it rains, small farm houses, grizzled farmers and short, round, but shockingly tough old ladies. Early on during my first visit, I saw an 80-something-year-old granny in full peasant, babushka regalia dragging a giant, fallen tree branch across her yard. I imagined she'd fetch a three-foot saw from the shed and cut the branch down to firewood to roast the pig she'd slaughtered barehanded at 5:00 a.m., before winning a head-butt battle with a goat in heat. But seriously, these are the toughest old ladies on Earth.

Arefu enjoys a very modest agro-tourism scheme. Many inhabitants claim to be direct descendents of the wily villagers who coordinated Dracula's escape from Poenari Castle in 1462. Though pretty much no one speaks English, or any other non-Romanian language, some homes in the village host travelers overnight. A modest flat rate gets you a serviceable, if not comfortable bed, full board, and nighttime entertainment including a bonfire, traditional live music, way too much fiery *ţuica* and, if there's a translator present, Dracula-centric storytelling.

If constant miscommunication and pooping in the garden aren't for you, you can find a few passable two-star hotels out by the main road.

After limping back to your car, consider visiting a few more attractions in the area, such as the Lake Vidraru Dam to the north. Here you can enjoy a vertigo-inducing look over the side, which comes with the bonus of learning how far your own vomit falls before vaporizing. Or, if you are as terrified of heights as I am, stand anywhere from 10 to 57 feet back from the edge—this is still a good view and is perfectly fine, so shut up.

This is only a warm up for the main event even farther north. After zigzagging through a thin, half-trashed forest road that threatens to shake loose the last bolt holding your muffler to your car, you'll encounter the beginning of the stupefying Transfăgărășan Road, Romania's highest asphalt road. This is an unforgettable driving experience— even behind the wheel of a gasping Dacia—winding over the stately Făgăraș Mountains, that connect Wallachia to Transylvania. Moreover, as you crawl up and down this monster, you can try to appreciate how grueling this trip must have been on horseback 600 years ago, particularly when done in hasty retreat, which our pal Dracula did at least once.

In 2009, the Top Gear boys tore up and down the Transfăgărășan Road in an Aston Martin DBS V12 Volante, a Ferrari California, and a Lamborghini Gallardo LP560-4 Spyder. Jeremy Clarkson, never one to shy away from definitive superlatives, giddily exclaimed, "This is the best road in the world!" Suffice to say, you should drive it if at all possible.

The road was born, not surprisingly, out of one of Nicolae Ceaușescu's many paranoid episodes, wanting to secure a Carpathian crossing in case of Russian invasion (as had happened in Czechoslovakia in 1968). Ceauşescu sent in the army to tackle the job, which they completed in a hectic four and a half years. Thirty-eight fall-down exhausted soldiers reportedly died of mishaps that occurred during construction and the road opened in September 1974.

Weather restricts access to the road from November through October. After climbing the brain-scrambling but mainly uneventful road on the south (Wallachia) side, you drive through a long tunnel and emerge on the north side, where, if you're like me, a creative mix of strung-together oh-wows and curse words will slip from your mouth.

Immediately on the right is Lake Bâlea. At an elevation of 2,034 meters (6,671 feet) above sea level, the lake is often lost in fog. I will save you the irritation of driving back and forth looking for the pathetic sign indicating the turn-off to the lake, like I did, and advise you to simply pull over when you see a lot of parked cars and roadside vendors selling corn on the cob. The walk from the road to the lake is about 15 minutes. Or drive it if you like, though with all the people wandering around driving is about as slow as walking. Plus, you run the risk of finding nowhere to park once you reach the busy lakeside chalet/restaurant. Assuming clear skies, it's unquestionably a worthwhile detour. If not, use your imagination and buy a postcard.

Back on the Transfăgărașan Road—even in a Dacia, the only compact car on Earth that coasts like a tank—you will barely touch the gas pedal while twisting down the north side of the mountain into Transylvania. The violent switchbacks take you past little waterfalls, fresh-fruit stands, and charming remote lodges. If you're driving alone, you'll just have to believe me about these pleasant views because taking your eyes off the road is suicide; guardrails range from pathetic to nonexistent.

Soon after descending below the tree line, you'll arrive at *Bâlea Cascada* (Bâlea Waterfall). This beauty is also frequently enshrouded in a fog so thick and creamy you could mix it in Parmesan and pour it over pasta. The walk to the waterfall isn't too far, so you can still get close for a photo even if there is fog. Also, the walk will help loosen your rapidly stiffening legs from the stairs workout back at Poenari.

-----------------------------------

The rebuilding of the highly strategic Poenari Castle did not go unnoticed by Dracula's foes. Though he had been biding his time and playing nice with both his new friends in Hungary and the increasingly testy Ottomans while he cleaned house in Wallachia, the building of this overtly defensive fortress violated his agreements with both parties. Dracula was going to have some 'splainin' to do.

But this was the 15th century, when months and even years passed between the planning and execution of large-scale invasions and revenge-fueled melees. Dracula had some time to kill, and what better way to kill time than killing a whole bunch of assholes getting up in his business?

Still in command of a sizable legion of mercenaries and troops, Dracula mustered his forces and headed into Transylvania to sort some stuff out with the people of Braşov.

# Braşov

Teutonic knights established Braşov, like most notable
sights in the area, in the 13th century on an ancient Dacian
settlement. Like Sighişoara, Braşov was a German Saxon
mercantile center settled by colonists invited by Hungary
and originally called Kronstadt (The City of the Crown). The
knights had been run off by 1225, but the Saxons and a
growing Hungarian population remained, developing Braşov
into one of the largest and richest cities in Transylvania. This
wealth was displayed in the form of huge, extravagant
churches and magnificent homes. Even before all this wealth
arrived, Braşov was attractive enough to be repeatedly
thrashed by Mongols and Turks, so one of the first things the
Saxons did was to begin constructing the mother of all city
walls, much of which still stands today.

Still, it wasn't all pimped out gold chalices, furs and
scepters for the people of Braşov. Outside the southwest
walls, the ethnic Romanians lived poor, powerless, and
discriminated against, bearing the brunt of many invasions
and sacking attempts by warriors attracted by the wealth
inside the walls. None other than our retribution-fueled
friend, Vlad Dracula, carried out what was probably the
most famous sacking of the city.

Riding the momentum of slaughtering past, present,
and maybe-possibly future enemies just in case, Dracula
stormed into Transylvania to creatively puncture a good

portion of Braşov's Saxon merchants. While Dracula may have been a little hasty about impaling some folks back in Wallachia, he had a legitimate beef with Braşov's aristocratic metrosexuals. They'd played a significant role in openly defying his authority, consorting with his enemies, and scheming to oust him from power and install Vladislav II, who you'll remember had recently been dispatched by Vlad while retaking his throne.

Vlad and his troops gathered at Bran Castle, Braşov's first line of defense against invaders approaching from the south. For whatever reason, on this occasion the guys on duty at Bran Castle apparently failed to prevent, or failed to try to prevent, this gang of armed and dangerous looters from marching on to Braşov[67]. In any case, Dracula soon arrived in Braşov, intent on breaching what was at the time one of Europe's best-defended towns.

The Saxons were probably feeling pretty confident about their chances against the upstart Prince, being that the city walls had grown to 14 feet thick in places and were fortified with well-outfitted defensive bastions, as well as towers from which defenders could unleash a hail of arrows, cannon, and musket fire on anyone who tried anything.

Since even Dracula wasn't crazy enough to attempt a standard frontal assault on the walls, he and his army hung back. They made the slightly less crazy decision to attack at night, plundering the inadequately fortified suburbs outside

---

[67] You had *one* job!

the city walls where, conveniently, noted rival Dan III's[68] court was located, along with many colluding boyars and hapless Romanians. Dan III and his court had been forewarned and fled[69], but Dracula consoled himself by slaughtering and impaling a good portion of the city's elite, allegedly thousands of people. He then burned the area to the ground.

He then successfully charged the city gates for a brief but undoubtedly terrifying round of additional massacring inside what locals believed to be an absolute safe zone. No doubt experiencing an intoxicating swoon after having unleashed so much pent-up desire for retribution, Dracula also made an ambitious attempt to burn down the Black Church, but Braşov's defensive forces finally coalesced and pushed Dracula's crew back into the forest.

It's said this is the episode when Vlad famously ate a meal while prisoners writhed on stakes in front of him, a scene depicted in a well-known etching. Indeed, it's highly likely this actually happened, since impaling people, especially in such heavy numbers, is remarkably intensive in terms of labor and time. Like anyone at any job, Vlad naturally needed to grab lunch at his "desk" as work continued around him. Legend also has it that Vlad, who

---

[68] Brother of former Wallachian Prince Vladislav II, recently laid out as a maggot buffet thanks to Dracula.

[69] Dan would later rally a group of allies, mainly people Dracula had wronged through destruction and the murdering of family members, for a showdown on the Transylvania-Wallachia border. Dan would lose the battle and be forced to dig his own grave before Dracula beheaded him.

allegedly gained confidence and apparently even a hearty appetite from seeing blood flow, dipped his bread into the blood of his victims as he ate. This incident was possibly absorbed during Bram Stoker's lengthy research and contributed to Dracula's evolution into a 19th-century vampire.

However, this event is also likely the source of the wildly exaggerated and therefore extremely popular German (Saxon) tales written about Vlad years and even decades later, stories that depict him as an unchained maniac rather than a warrior who was just slightly more sadistic than his peers. Dazed and traumatized survivors of Dracula's attacks had made their way west and provided German writers with source material that portrayed him as a character in horror stories while he was still alive, escalating him to a full-blown demon in later decades. These stories depicted a crazed beast who ate human body parts and drank blood. Vlad was guilty of many horrifying things—no denying that—but apart from these stories, there is no evidence that he was cannibalistic.

Nonetheless, these stories, both true and exaggerated, came in handy when (spoiler alert) Hungary needed evidence to defend their withdrawal of support for Dracula and Matthias Corvinus started taking heat from the rest of Europe for locking up the Prince in Buda, which we'll learn more about later.

Having emphatically made his opinions clear on the subject of Saxons getting up in his business, Dracula departed a still-smoking Braşov, presumably carting off enough coin to keep his army of mercenaries happy as well as finance the massive fortress he would soon build in Bucharest.

Ethnic Romanians would go on to live as second-class citizens for centuries. Braşov was occupied by Romanian troops in WWI and, along with all of Transylvania, joined the Kingdom of Romania in 1918. After that, everyone in Braşov—Saxons *and* Romanians—was loving life as the city prospered for three decades until WWII. The anti-German backlash at the end of the war resulted in huge numbers of Braşov's Saxons being shipped off to the Soviet Union for what must have been a highly unpleasant and short remainder of their lives. Those who somehow avoided this fate later emigrated to West Germany when Romania went Communist.

------------------------------------------

Dracula's association with the city of Braşov ended 500 years ago with his prompting of mass bladder failure and the robbing and staking of Braşov's elite. But even a dedicated Dracula tourist should spend a few days in Braşov, arguably Romania's top tourism destination. I've been there something like six times and have never tired of it.

The city is ringed by mountains and lushly forested hills, one of which, Mount Tampa, shoots up just outside the southeast walls and features a Hollywood-style "Braşov" sign. City planners thought this was such a good idea that they tore it down and built an even bigger one in the mid-

2000s. It's possible to walk up there, or take a cable car, to enjoy great views of the city and perhaps a meal in a communist-era restaurant.

Between 1950 and 1960, because all kinds of wacky Russia ass-kissing was going on anyway, Braşov was charmingly renamed "Oraşul Stalin" ("Stalin City"). Then they deforested Stalin's name into the side of Mount Tampa for good measure. Keeping with the Stalin theme, this was when crazed industrialization really took off in Braşov and the Romanian government forced thousands of stunned and unprepared villagers to move from the countryside into the city in order to fill those factories.

The city sprawls today, including large areas still devoted to the churning—though declining—heavy manufacturing industry. But down in the southwest corner sits Piaţa Sfantului (Council Square), the center of Braşov's walled Old Town and, after Sibiu, Romania's prettiest square in my opinion.

The square is surrounded by baroque facades with arched doorways that were once merchants' shops and are now almost all patio-ed restaurants and cafés. The centerpiece, which is decidedly off-center, is the Council House (*Casa Sfatului*), first built in the 13th century[70], all yellow with an orange-tiled roof and topped by a combination clock tower and trumpeter's tower. Today it anticlimactically doubles as a tourist information center and

---

[70] The current edifice dates from 1420.

the Braşov Historical Museum, with exhibits on the history of Braşov's Saxon guilds and a half-hearted torture room. But for centuries Braşov's councilors, more regally known as "centurions," assembled here, fretting about trade profit margins and, on several occasions, actively scheming to sabotage that pain-in-the-ass (literally) Prince Vlad Dracula.

The square footage of the structure that wasn't devoted to council frowning was used to torture assorted deserving and/or hapless individuals. When space didn't permit, they took the show to the square outside, including what is claimed to be the last documented witch-burning in Europe[71]. For the record, two other witch trials conducted on the down-low, as witchcraft had ceased to be recognized as a criminal offense, in Switzerland (1782) and Prussia (1811) also make this claim. The council house is said to be haunted, of course.

The *actual* center of the square has a '70s-era, Soviet-inspired water fountain. On the southeast side of the square is the massive, Renaissance Hirscher House, a.k.a. the "Merchants House," constructed and opened in 1539-45. Today it houses a restaurant, a pleasant art gallery, and other businesses, but it used to be a space where merchants could retreat to do business during inclement weather. It was financed by Apollonia Hirscher, in memory of her deceased husband and former town mayor, Lucas Hirscher.

---

[71] A factoid listed in my Lonely Planet and, as such, repeated a thousand times elsewhere.

Peeking out over the buildings on the square's south side is the massive Black Church (*Biserica Neagră*), which is allegedly the largest Gothic church in Southeastern Europe[72]. Work on this monster began in 1383 on the site of a previous church that had been destroyed during a 13th-century Mongol invasion. Due to several setbacks, including extensive damage during an Ottoman raid in 1421, the church wasn't completed until 1480.

It wasn't inaugurated as the "Black Church," of course—that would've been creepy, even by medieval standards. Rather, it got its name from a 1689 fire that charred the structure inside and out. Confusingly, the church isn't black anymore. The structure got a vigorous scrub-down a few years back, removing all the layers of soot that had given it its nickname.

Still discernable on the outside of the church are conspicuous gouges in the stone walls. Depending on whom you talk to, these were either caused by medieval soldiers sharpening their swords or butchers sharpening their cleavers. If you're wondering why the base seems so disproportionately large, as with many funds-starved construction projects in Romania, the original designs had the bell tower being much larger, but they ran out of cash and had to build a budget-priced bell tower.

---

[72] I've only spent a few moments trying to fact check this item, but it seems to be a legit claim.

Once you're inside the bright, baroque church and have taken a few moments to absorb its stained glass windows and massive columns, turn around and look up. Those statues were once on the outside of the church on the apse, but were moved inside for protection from the elements. Hanging from the balconies on both sides of the congregation are about 120 traditional, ornate Turkish rugs[73], acquired and brought back by merchants from risky business trips into Ottoman territory during the 17th and 18th centuries, which they donated to the church as thanks to God for allowing them to return home with all their body parts still in their correct places. Make a wish and drop a coin through the wooden grates in the floor, if that's your thing.

The church's main attraction is the 4,000-pipe organ, built by Buchholz of Berlin in 1839, which is said to be the only still-functioning Buchholz that has been preserved in its original form. Some keyboard wizard performs organ recitals in the church Tuesdays, Thursdays and Saturdays at 6:00 p.m. in July and August only, as has been tradition since 1891.

Fans of tourist shtick will want to wander one block south, toward Mount Tampa and locate the cobbled, pedestrian-only *Strada Storii* (Rope Street), which, as a handy plaque explains, has a width of just 1.32 meters (just

---

[73] Even in the damn 17th-century, you couldn't walk through a Turkish market without being pounced on and suffering a hard-sell for a rug.

over four feet), making it one of Europe's narrowest streets. At the far end of Storii, zigzag a few blocks farther south until you home in on the conspicuous cable car terminal that creaks up Mount Tampa. People who prefer to earn their high up views through pain and perspiration can also trudge up to the viewing area via a few winding trails in about an hour.

In addition to the "Braşov" sign and viewing platform with the best up-high views of the city, Mount Tampa also features that Soviet-era restaurant, mentioned earlier, which stands on the site of Braşov's first defensive fortress—and many fortress iterations thereafter. One of the early structures was set upon and heavily damaged by a rampaging Vlad Ţepeş in 1458, who, upon further reflection, had the whole thing torn down in 1460, impaling about 40 merchants in the process for form's sake. A new wooden structure was built in 1524, and then rebuilt in more resilient stone later in the 16th century. Barely a century later, cannon technology had become so destructively advanced that the fortress was deemed a flimsy death box, so it was abandoned.

The north side of Piaţa Sfantului drains into the pedestrian-only, entertainment-focused Strada Republicii, where shopping, evening strolling, and decent, if pricey, eating and drinking can be found. At the far end is the somber wooden-cross memorial to the victims of the 1989 Revolution.

Many sections of Old Braşov's hefty 15th-century defensive wall are still standing, as well as a few defensive towers and gates. Work to build and fortify the walls went on from 1400 to 1650, peaking with the walls reaching 40 feet high in some places, as many as seven feet thick, and two miles long.

In the 19th-century, when urban sprawl became more inconvenient than invasions and sackings, much of the wall was pulled down, but substantial sections have been preserved. Among these surviving fragments are a few of the seven original defensive bastions, which, like in Sighie, were maintained by guilds, including the Weavers' Bastion (*Bastionul Tesatorilor*), on the wall's southeast corner. Impressively large as bastions go, the 15th-century structure also contains the Weavers' Bastion Museum (*Muzeul Bastionul Tesatorilor*), which is inside a building that also dates back to the 15th century. The exhibits are a bit underwhelming, though it does feature an elaborate model of 17th century Braşov made in 1896 by a German schoolteacher.

On the southwestern side of the Old Town is the pentagon-shaped, three-level Blacksmith's Bastion (*Bastionul Fierarilor*), dating from 1529 and home to the Braşov Archives, consisting of over 100,000 ancient documents. Among these are 80 letters spanning from the 14th to 16th century, plus what is allegedly the oldest surviving letter written in the Romanian language, scribbled out in 1521 by one Neacsu[74], a merchant from Campulung.

Also worthwhile is the Graft Bastion (*Bastionul Graft*), on the west side of the city, dating from 1521 and recently restored. Inside the bastion is a claustrophobic, four-level structure with a variety of medieval artifacts on display. Outside is a bit of a puzzle. Though I'm sure this wasn't a feature of the original bastion, at some point some idiot incorporated a defensively dubious arch built outward from the bastion, acting as a portal for the path leading around the exterior of the wall. Call me crazy, but that seems like a great place to lurk and launch a surprise attack when someone opens the back door to empty out the chamber pot. Or, even easier, a convenient place to start a ruinous bonfire.

The best vantage point for wall examination is on the western side of the city, along a stream on Strada Dupa Ziduri. About 200 steps above this section of the wall on the hillside are the Black Tower (*Turnul Neagru*) and White Tower (*Turnul Alba*), both dating from 1494—confusingly white, incidentally. These squat buildings are "towers" only in the sense that they were considered tall in the 15th-century. One can enter and climb to the tops of both towers for panoramic photos of the city.

For a taste of how the 99 percent lived during Saxon times, head to the southwest edge of Old Braşov, through Schei Gate into the Schei District. Romanians were not only banned from owning property inside the walled portion of

---

[74] Apparently there weren't enough people in that era for last names to be necessary.

the city until the 17<sup>th</sup> century, but those who wanted to sell merchandise could enter the city only during specific periods (and only after paying a fee). So, the Romanian community clustered in Schei, living in humble homes and, of course, virtually defenseless during routine raids by invaders. Several centuries-old homes in the neighborhood have been preserved.

Today the Schei District is more well-to-do in terms of property prices, but still medieval in virtually every other aspect. Houses are still mostly tiny, many made of brick or stone and covered in a painted cement skin, with weathered wooden window shutters on the ground floor and peep-hole windows on the first level. Others are modern, though still small, built with what seems to have been a passing attempt at preserving a bit of the classic design, such as faux-clay roof tiles. Streets remain narrow and haphazard, very likely spontaneously plotted out wherever there was space wide enough between structures to accommodate a horse-drawn cart. Modern cars can navigate the area just fine, with only the occasional meeting of two cars on a single-lane stretch, sitting nose-to-nose in a test of wills to see who will reverse and let the other through.

Once you've absorbed the top-shelf attractions, Braşov has enough ancient churches and so-so museums to keep you busy for several days. Or, as most do, you can use Braşov as a staging area for a few day trips.

-------------------------------------

As mentioned above, a veritable conga line of buses, mini-buses, trains and rental cars fills the roads and rails to the southwest of Braşov, passing by Râşnov at 18 kilometers (11 miles), and Bran at 27 kilometers (17 miles).

Do whatever you like, but I would stop in Râşnov first, so as not to upset the Rule of Escalating Amazingness™, being that Râşnov Fortress, wonderful as it is, will not have quite the same oh-wow factor as Bran Castle. Half restored, half ruins, the hilltop 13th-century fortress (*Cetatea Râşnov*), when last I checked, wasn't nearly as tourist-choked as Bran, so it's a good way to ease into a day of sightseeing really old stuff. If you choose the other way around, depending on the season, you risk missing Râşnov, because after a visit to Bran you're just gonna want a nap—or a bar.

There's parking available up the hill and closer to the fortress entrance, but people arriving by public transport will be dropped at or near Râşnov town's Piaţa Unirii. From there it's a modestly challenging 15-minute walk up the steps to the fortress. Don't worry about finding it; the fortress is massive and utterly conspicuous up on the hill there, though some town mayor, in what was likely a fit of sign-envy with Braşov, installed a hillside "Râşnov" sign below the fortress for good measure.

The fortress was another project started by those prolific Teutonic Knights as a line of defense against Tartar, and later, Turkish attacks. The walls eventually grew to be five meters (16 feet) tall and up to 1.5 meters (4.9 feet) thick in places. The south, north, and west sides of the citadel are built up to the edge of sharp 150-meter (490-foot) cliffs, which would be treacherous to climb even without the threat of falling arrows and stones. The more accessible east side is the most heavily fortified, protected by a double-gate, double tower-entrance design with a courtyard between the gates and towers. Surrounded by balconies, this is presumably where invaders would be trapped without cover and easily snuffed had they managed to breach the first gate.

The timing of Râşnov's construction was exquisite. Just after the fortress was completed in 1335, the Tartars rolled up with foul intent and Râşnov successfully outlasted the siege. It's said to have withstood three Ottoman sieges, including an especially tenacious and failed effort in 1421. In fact, the fortress was occupied only once, in 1612, when invaders found and blocked the path to the fortress' water source. Despite sustaining heavy damage from a fire (1718) and an earthquake (1802), the fortress remained in some manner of use until it was finally abandoned in 1850, after it had served as refuge for nearby villagers one last time while Hungarian revolutionaries and Austrian imperial troops galloped through the area. A desperately needed, though rudimentary restoration was carried out in 1955-56. Further restorations have occurred in stages as funds became available, the most recent taking place in 2010.

Though someone came to their senses years ago and carted away the disappointingly out-of-place wooden Count Dracula statue selfie station, you can still find a number of places to pose for Facebook fodder, such as the hanging shackles in the main courtyard. Judging by the "Keep off the grass" sign (which is in Romanian, obvs) you should probably resist the urge to insert yourself (or a sibling) into the wooden prisoner stocks, lest you be screamed at by one of the aunties tending the grounds.

Like many fortresses back in olden times, Râşnov was put into use as a refuge for the people of the nearby villages so frequently, and for such long intervals, that it eventually evolved into a small, extremely well-defended gated community. Roughly 30 stone dwellings, some of them now restored, were built to house villagers and their property during sieges, including special tiled roofs resistant to catapulted firebombs. You'll need at least an hour to wander the grounds, travel up and down the steep alleys, and check out the restored structures, tiny cottages thoughtfully outfitted with window flower boxes, a variety of wagons and sleds of varying ages, and of course the massive walls and iron gates. The 146-meter (479-foot), 17th-century well, built after the 1612 defeat due to that water-source fiasco, is said to have been dug by two Turkish prisoners who were motivated by the promise of freedom after they finished. This task allegedly took 17 years[75].

You can actually enter the church as well as the jail, and there you should take a moment to peek into the cell below the barred hole in the floor, which appears to contain

---

[75] What, were they digging with spoons?

genuine human remains. Finally there's the matter of taking, let's see here, about 27 panoramic photos (if you're like me) of the nearby countryside and mountains from the top of the walls. There's also a small museum with some R-Rated prints of torture, medieval weapons, tools, stamps, and other paraphernalia.

-------------------------------

The other top daytrip out of Braşov is Poiana Braşov, a well-regarded skiing destination in winter and a jaw-slackening hiking spot the rest of the year. Poiana Braşov is about 16 bendy, uphill kilometers (10 miles) south of Braşov, sitting at roughly 1,030 meters (3,380 feet) above sea level on the backside of the Bucegi Mountains. It was long considered an over-hyped ski area, often disappointing tourists who had already been to genuinely exceptional ski resorts elsewhere in Europe. Word about its many, over-priced failings finally became so widespread that they threw some money at it in the early 2010s, including elongating the 10 main slopes from a cumulative 13.8 (8.6 miles) to 23.9 kilometers (14.9 miles). This massive upgrade won them the hosting privileges for the 2013 European Youth Olympic Winter Festival.

Outside the ski season (which is roughly from December to March), hiking trails spider out from high up the Postavaru Massif down into Cheii Valley, Timisului Valley and Poiana Braşov resort. If you'd like, head farther up the mountain on a three-hour trudge to Cristianul Mare, the massif's highest peak. Trails of moderate difficulty will take you down to Timisu de Jos and Timisu de Sus (three or four hours depending on your pace) where you can catch a train back to Braşov. Or just walk back to Braşov over the top of Mount Tampa, like a badass. Alternatively, if you're feeling hella-badass, you can set off from Braşov nice and early, hike over Mount Tampa and through Poiana Braşov to Râşnov Fortress in two to three hours, then take a bus to Bran then back to Braşov, though that sounds like a sadistically long day.

People wanting to forgo the sweat and grime but still looking to bask in the splendor of the Carpathian Mountains can hop on the year-round cable car service up to the Cristianu Mare and Postăvaru peaks.

Poiana Braşov is a quick bus ride from Braşov, with runs departing about every 30 minutes.

---------------------------------------

Braşov and its regional environs may not be a vampire and paranormal monster hotspot, but worry not, there's still a chance here, however small, of being chomped on, disemboweled and/or bled dry. Among Ceauşescu's less disastrous legacies are the consequences of banning bear hunting in Romania[76]. Without any predators, the brown bear population in Romania has grown to an estimated 6,000—said to be 60 percent of Europe's entire bear population—many of which are running around the outskirts of Braşov and nearby mountains.

---

[76] Though Nicolae himself was allowed to shoot them at will, of course.

Why would normally human-averse bears linger so close to one of Romania's biggest cities? Two reasons: One, they've figured out they can get easy meals by rummaging through the city's dumpsters. Two, some tourism agencies in town run "bear tours," which in some irresponsible cases involves setting out bait so bears make an appearance and please the tour groups. This has naturally caused the bears to form the dangerous association that humans = food. Bear attacks happen routinely enough to have become a legitimate problem. These incidents usually involve hikers in the mountains who accidentally sneak up and startle bears, who, like humans when confronted by especially large spiders, scream like children and then use whatever's handy to smash them into a pile of mangled limbs. But there have been urban attacks as well, including one guy who was "ripped to shreds" while sleeping on a park bench, as well as a policeman killed by a bear outside a mountain village. A bear attack story in or around Braşov makes the international news about once a year.

Speaking of running, did you know brown bears can run up to 30 MPH? I don't care how fast you run scared, that bear is going to catch your ass. So, if you're hiking or camping in the area, use your outside voice loudly and continuously, even if you're alone, so the bears know you're there. Also, pitch your tents in a large clearing, so there's no chance *they* will accidentally sneak up on *you*, in which case you still lose[77].

---------------------------------

Even though Braşov is *the* place virtually every tourist in Romania must visit, with crowds getting pretty heavy in summer, the Old Town is still quite peaceful and locals seem to be unfazed by the constant influx of staggering, camera-distracted tourists. Part of what has kept Braşov from becoming a full-blown tourist-saturated hellhole is its lack of an airport. To get here, you've got to fly into Bucharest or Sibiu and submit to a dues-earning, mystifyingly slow train ride for 150-some kilometers (93 miles). But that's all about to change.

After some start-stop contract troubles, Braşov's new airport construction is in full swing. In fact, at the time of this writing, the runway is already complete. All it needs is a terminal, which is rumored to be designed to handle one million passengers per year. That's a shitload of tourists for Braşov's diminutive historic center to somehow absorb. Direct flights to and from London, Paris, and other points in Western Europe tend to attract the bachelor/bachelorette party crowd, which seems to jump from one Eastern European city to the next as prices rise and the crowds shift to the next dirt-cheap locale. Braşov will have to work very hard to keep their town from turning into the next Bratislava.

---

[77] Your face.

# Bucharest

Newly flush with cash after sacking Braşov, Dracula galloped to what is now Bucharest to build the last of his defensive fortresses aimed at stopping, or at least temporarily kind of slowing down, the Ottoman tsunami[78] that would soon wash over Wallachia like, well, like a super angry tsunami.

Though Wallachia's southern frontier was, as it is now, the imposing, challenging-to-cross, natural defensive line that is the Danube River, Vlad chose to position his stronghold a couple dozen miles north on the Dâmboviţa River, which I'm sure made some kind of tactical sense at the time.

Over one thousand workers and stonemasons threw the massive fortress together in what was astounding speed for the era, saving themselves a lot of backbreaking digging by building on the foundation of previous fortresses.

The actual name "Bucharest" was in use almost immediately after completion of the fortress, first appearing as "Citadel of Bucureşti" in documents dating from 1459. The area, already a center for merchants and craftsmen since the beginning of the 1400s, blossomed as the fortress evolved from a stronghold into a regional center of commerce and power. Unlike those pompous Saxon ass-hats in Transylvania trying to hoard all the wealth for themselves, in Bucharest the Romanian, Austrian, Greek, Bulgarian,

---

[78] And yes, that would be an outstanding band name. You're welcome.

Serbian, Armenian and Jewish mingled and conducted business freely, setting up their shops and doing brisk trade. The Germans were present, too. In fact the area eventually became known as "Lipscani," for all the German traders hailing from Lipsca or Leipzig. The neighborhood north of the Princely Court is still known as Lipscani today, filled with art galleries, antique shops, coffeehouses, bars, clubs and live-music venues.

After trading the title of "Princely Court" with Târgoviște a couple of times, Bucharest finally became the permanent capital of Wallachia under Constantin Brâncoveanuin in 1698.

After Dracula's death, the Ottoman Empire eventually triumphed and added the formidable fortress in Bucharest, as well as all of Wallachia, to their ever-growing map of principalities. Though Wallachia kept its autonomy and even maintained successive Wallachian princes as figureheads, the Ottomans appointed Greek administrators to effectively run Bucharest, as per the usual arrangement when the Ottoman Empire absorbed a new territory. This no doubt maddening arrangement would persist until a short but productive revolt in 1821 resulted in the Greeks being relieved of their administrative duties, though Romania was not completely free of the Turkish yoke until 1877.

-------------------------------------------------

The 17th and 18th centuries weren't exactly a cakewalk for anyone in Europe, but Bucharest was particularly beset by calamity. The city was half destroyed and rebuilt several times during a series of natural disasters over 200 years. Then a bubonic plague known as "Caragea's plague" arrived in Bucharest, traveling up through Ottoman territory via Istanbul (again), claiming 20,000-30,000 lives in 1813–14, a significant portion of the city's 120,000 citizens. Then a cholera epidemic landed on the city (because of course), draining Bucharest's population to just 60,000, according to a demoralizing 1831 census.

On top of all that unpleasantness, throughout this period Bucharest was the juicy bone in a three-way dogfight between the Ottomans, the Habsburgs, and the Russians. Though the Ottomans always came out on top, eventually, Bucharest was occupied by the Habsburgs in 1716, 1737, and 1789, and Imperial Russia on three separate occasions between 1768 and 1806. One can only imagine the political and cultural whiplash everyday citizens went through during this period, though undertakers got rich, I bet.

The Ottoman Empire's slow-motion loss of control over Bucharest started in 1828 when Russia, after yet another occupation, formally placed the city under its administration. And because no catastrophes had occurred for a while, naturally the universe dick-punched Bucharest again, this time with a fire that destroyed about 2,000 buildings (roughly one third of the city) on March 23, 1847.

Still smoking a little from that fire, Bucharest somehow found the wherewithal to launch the Wallachian Revolution in 1848, which resulted in the region getting its first taste of true freedom and legitimate domestic rule in centuries. Alas, it didn't take long for Russia to regain control. But the Russians were once again chased out of Wallachia and Moldavia in 1854 during the Crimean War, which started a new game of musical chairs between aspirant controlling entities. This period included an extended occupation of Bucharest by Austrian forces, who sat on the city until March 1857 while Vienna tried to figure out the lesser of two evils between Ottoman versus Russian rule so close to home. Despite being square in the thick of it, Austria ultimately remained neutral throughout the Crimean War.

A flurry of pivotal historical events took place in the 20 years between 1859 and 1878. Bucharest's ego took a hit when the Moldavian city of Iaşi was declared the capital after Wallachia and Moldavia joined in 1859 and started calling themselves the Romanian United Principalities. It was only a brief affront, however, as power was transferred back to Bucharest in 1862. After a palace coup against Romania's first leader Alexandru Ioan Cuza in 1866, Prussian Prince Carol of Hohenzollern-Sigmaringen, backed by Romania's important ally Prussia, was elected ruler.

A war of independence in 1877-78 ensued, with Romania joining forces with Russia during the Russo-Turkish War to eject the Ottoman Empire once and for all. Romania was granted independence under the 1878 Treaty of Berlin, a victory that included some tense land negotiations and strained relations with their new pal Russia, where Romania gained Northern Dobrogea (securing expanded access to the Black Sea) in exchange for southern Bessarabia[79]. In 1881, Romania declared itself a kingdom, with the former Carol of Hohenzollern-Sigmaringen getting promoted to King Carol I.

The Kingdom of Romania had a promising start. Bucharest's population mushroomed, and the city embarked on a period of rapid urban development and wealth accumulation, including the introduction of gas lighting, horse-drawn trams and even some electrification. The flood-prone Dâmbovița River was channeled in 1883, and the fortifications of Bucharest were built. A "golden age" of ornate, Western Europe-influenced architecture gave the city a vitalizing, cosmopolitan air, namely prominent street Calea Victoriei being redeveloped in the spirit of the Champs-Élysées, which inspired people to start ambitiously referring to Bucharest as the "Little Paris" (*Micul Paris*) of the east[80].

Calea Victoriei was originally built in 1692, laid with oak beams, smoothing the spine-decalcifying dirt track linking the Old Princely Court to Mogosoaia Palace. The street got its modern name in 1878 to mark Romania's victory in the War of Independence. Architects Horia Creangă and Marcel Iancu, whose preferences leaned toward

---

[79] Located in northern Romania, territory which is now mainly in the Republic of Moldova with bits spilling over into Ukraine.

[80] A moniker that would continue to be used long after its relevance had faded under Ceaușescu's systematic destruction of large parts of historic Bucharest.

Modern (a.k.a. "Rationalist") Architecture, drove this period of giddy development.

During World War I, the Battle of Bucharest ended with German occupation of the city enduring from December 6, 1916, to November 1918, during which time the government and what was left of Romania's armed forces retreated and reestablished the capital in Iaşi. After WWI, Bucharest once again became the capital of the newly engorged Greater Romania[81]. Bucharest flourished during the interwar years, with an average of 30,000 new residents arriving in the city each year, the further Champs-Élysées-ification of Calea Victoriei, and the construction of Palatul Telefoanelor.

However, Romania's tendency for misfortune soon returned. The Great Depression hit the city especially hard, then things took a turn for the horrific during WWII[82]. Despite being allied with Germany, Romania's Conducător[83], Ion Antonescu, wasn't convinced that allowing the enthusiastically fascist and pain-in-his-ass Iron Guard[84] to indiscriminately attack and loot Jewish families was the best use of government resources. He began working to reduce

---

[81] Despite getting their asses kicked, Romania came out of the war with a bunch of new territory, including Transylvania, Crişana, Banat and Bukovina.

[82] Which isn't to say that anything about WWII *wasn't* horrific, but you know what I mean, dude.

[83] Leader.

[84] Basically a nationalistic, extremely violent, anti-Semitic, well-armed version of America's hateful Tea Party, which flourished in Romania from 1927 into the early part of World War II.

the group's political power, prompting a large contingent to rebel. The three-day melee that ensued in January 1941 is known today as the Legionnaires' rebellion and Bucharest pogrom. The Iron Guard killed 125 Jews and 30 government soldiers, causing so much destabilizing chaos that even Hitler grew uneasy[85]. Government forces eventually stomped the rebellion, killing about 200 Legionnaires in the process and imprisoning another 9,000[86].

Bucharest took it on the chin again in WWII. Being the capital of an Axis country and a major transit point for Axis troops, the city was hammered by Allied bombings. After the royal coup on August 23, 1944, when allegiance switched to the Allies, Bucharest again was the subject of bombings, this time by the Nazis' Luftwaffe, followed by street skirmishes as Germany tried and failed to retake the city.

Miraculously, the city recovered well after WWII, even with communism taking hold, though it should be noted that this period kicked off the urgent construction of charmless, slapdash, cement apartment blocks, which are a blight on cities across Romania to this day. Then Nicolae Ceaușescu took power and Bucharest, along with all of

---

[85] You know you've gone *way* off the reservation when your antics are so rowdy that even Hitler's like "Guys, guys, take it easy. It's not a race, mkay?"

[86] Though weakened, the Iron Guard was nonetheless able to stage the Iași pogrom in June and July of that same year, which was among the most vicious pogroms in Jewish history. With the help of German troops, over 13,000 Jews were murdered.

Romania, went right to shit, including the systematic destruction of much of the city's historic center to make room for still more god-awful urban development. The crowning blunder of this ill-considered redevelopment came late in Ceaușescu's rule when work began on the megalomaniac, fever-dream eyesore, the Palace of the Parliament which remains the world's largest civilian building and can probably be seen from a low orbit.

Yet more buildings in Bucharest's historic center were damaged or destroyed by an earthquake on March 4, 1977, the epicenter just 135 kilometers (83.89 miles) away, claiming 1,500 lives.

As Romania spiraled into abject debt, Ceaușescu's grand urban design for Bucharest slowed to a crawl. It took more than a decade after the 1989 Revolution for the economy to recover enough for significant city planning and construction to resume. The city started its slow transformation to more modern architecture and urban renewal around 2000, which continues today. Walk half a mile and you'll likely see buildings ranging from neo-classical, Bauhaus and art deco, and the ever-present communist-era gray apartment blocks, to modern steel and glass. Commercial development has kicked into high gear along with desperately needed repairs and upgrades to the street and road infrastructure. Restoration of Bucharest's historic center inched forward with agonizing slowness, particularly in the Lipscani district where it sometimes seemed months would go by without a single shovel of dirt being moved. Once completed, Lipscani thrived as a nightlife and entertainment district, a reputation still intact today, though the hip kids have begun to disperse to newer, trendier locales around the city.

------------------------------------

Bucharest has long had a bad reputation for being some kind of crime-ridden hellhole. It may be a hellhole in some ways, but crime is not one of them. Violent crime has always been pretty rare—so rare, in fact, that instances of it usually made headline news. Wanting to buff their crime reputation's wax job further during their consideration for EU membership[87], Romania rounded up large numbers of the once formidable mafia, which, for a while, reduced the already low rate of violent crime to something approaching Vatican City levels.

I actually witnessed one of these blink-and-it's-over mafia arrest maneuvers while I was living in Iași in 2004. Hearing a screeching of tires outside my apartment window, I peered out just in time to see four SWAT-like officers, complete with black ski masks, leap out of a police van, snatch a guy off a street corner, toss him into the vehicle and squeal away. A fifth officer recorded the entire operation on video for some reason. The whole thing took maybe 10 seconds.

What Romania *does* struggle with, however, is petty crime, particularly pickpocketing and a fading but still

---

[87] Which they gained in a photo-finish decision in 2007.

present element of confidence schemes, mainly targeting tourists.

A 2011 census tallied 1,883,425 inhabitants within Bucharest's city limits. Compared to other European capitals and/or cities of the same size, Bucharest's crime rate remains extremely low. Reported offenses declined by 51 percent between 2000 and 2004, then dropped another seven percent between 2012 and 2013. Violent crime fell by 13 percent in 2013 compared to the previous year, though there was a slight uptick in murders, which numbered 19[88].

------------------------------------

Dracula's fortress, today known as the Old Princely Court (*Curtea Veche*), became the cornerstone for what is now the city of Bucharest. The Old Court went through several iterations and expansions after Vlad's short, hyper-productive tenure as the fortress' master. Its first rehab occurred after it sustained significant damage during a siege shortly after Vlad's death. It was greatly expanded by Prince Mircea Ciobanul (Mircea the Shepherd), who somehow found time for redecorating during his sporadic rule (1545-1552, 1553-1554, and 1558-1559). At the time, all these fortress improvements may have seemed more like a paranoid vanity project than strictly for defense as Wallachia had long since been leashed by the Ottoman Empire, but

---

[88] Show me a city of two million in the U.S. with fewer than 19 murders in a year and I'll eat this book or Kindle or whatever.

even the mighty Ottomans had trouble keeping Bucharest locked down, as you'll remember from a few pages back.

Matei Basarab rebuilt the palace during his reign (1632-1654), making it "amazingly elegant" with a "charming aspect, much finer and gayer," according to a breathless visitor of the time. The complex went full-Liberace gay during yet another enlargement a century later, directed by Prince Constantin Brancoveanu (ruled 1688-1714), whose contributions included a magnificent marble staircase inside the entrance.

The complex suffered a slow, ungraceful demise after a series of fires in the 19th century, leading to abandonment and neglect. Subsequent earthquakes and looting for building materials all but leveled what was left.

Ruins of the complex, discovered during an archeological dig in 1967, opened as a museum in 1972 and very recently underwent a renovation and beautification project. Some remnants of the 15th-century walls and arches are intact, as well as the palace throne room. The exterior of the fortress ruins isn't particularly awe-inspiring. Only a single level remains above ground, with artifacts haphazardly scattered about such as tombstones, bits and pieces of Corinthian columns (including one that has been laboriously reassembled with the help of a lot of cement), and a bust of Dracula himself of unknown age or origin out front.

Inside, one can view Dacian pottery, Roman coins and the oldest surviving document mentioning the city of

Bucharest, written in Slavonic[89], dated September 20, 1459, and signed by Vlad himself. It's possible to tour large sections of the excavated and impressively intact cellars, which allegedly once fanned out beneath much of Old Bucharest. The cellars also contained dungeons, where Vlad tossed prisoners for what were undoubtedly unpleasant and brief stays before death's sweet, sweet embrace.

Also on the site are the more substantial ruins of the Old Court Church (*Biserica Curtea Veche*), built on orders of Mircea the Shepherd[90] in 1559, making it the oldest surviving church in Bucharest. The church served as the coronation spot for Romania's princes for some 200 years.

Because princes couldn't just sit there and appreciate what they had in those days, the church was enlarged in 1715 by Ştefan Cantacuzino. One can still view a variety of the church's interior frescoes, including some 16th-century originals near the altar, with additional frescoes dating from 1847. The church's exterior was also scrubbed down during the recent renovation.

A bit of fun, modern trivia: The Old Princely Court was where an already harried Anthony Bourdain had a meltdown during his ill-fated and only visit to Romania in 2008. Admittedly, the maddening, everyday bureaucracy and unconcealed profiteering off foreigners in Romania would probably drive a nun to throw her poop at the Pope,

---

[89] A Slavic liturgical language used by the Orthodox Church, mainly in Eastern Europe.
[90] Who is, in fact, buried there.

but the "No Reservations" folks made the mystifying decision to let their Russian pal Zamir be their tour guide and fixer in Romania. Zamir was a frequent guest on the show and had previously led the crew through successful trips to Uzbekistan and Russia. However, the fact that he apparently spoke no Romanian and had seemingly visited the country once in the 90s didn't seem like a red flag to anyone.

It's unclear what the exact chronology of their visit was, or what unpleasantness they had already suffered, but in the episode itself Bourdain's crew rocked up to the Old Princely Court first thing. In the scene, Bourdain is already mumbling darkly about bureaucratic nonsense and Romania's "struggle against tourism," so it's likely that other injustices had already been endured off camera; in short, Bourdain appears to be one inconvenience away from head-butting a church.

Despite having permission to film at the Court from some high office, the guards that day must have picked up the scent of U.S. television network travel budgets and decided to execute a scam—an asinine scam, but a scam nonetheless. After a brief huddle, the guards demanded that the crew pay "10 euros per meter" to film at the Court. What the fuck that even means is anyone's guess, but Bourdain stormed away before anyone could recover their wits to ask for clarification about the nonsensical shakedown attempt.

From there, Anthony went from inconsolable to despondent. The hapless Zamir led him from one unfortunate and humiliating experience to another, and then the intrepid guide hit the țuica hard after hurting his back during a failed attempt at a humorous scene driving a half-busted Dacia 1310. It seems the only saving grace of the visit was several fortifying helpings of pork[91].

To be fair, the "No Reservations" crew produced a lot of outstanding travel TV over the years, with only a few notable fuck-ups, but this one was exceptional and a huge letdown to the can't-catch-a-break country of Romania.

Near the Old Princely Court is Manuc's Inn (*Hanul lui Manuc*), originally built by a successful Armenian trader by the name of Emanuel Marzaian between 1804 and 1808. Intended as a place for local tradesmen to chillax or travelers to rest during their journeys from the Balkans and Turkey into Europe, it was unquestionably upscale and swank. In fact, preliminary talks for the peace treaty that ended the Russian-Turkish War were held at the inn in 1812, and peace treaties are almost never hammered out in flea-bitten dumps[92].

By the mid-1800s, the inn had developed into a kind of business center with 107 spots for tenants and offices, including 15 wholesalers, 23 retail stores, a couple of receiving rooms and a pub. It also briefly served as Bucharest's town hall in 1842, a theater sometime around 1880, and once again played a part in history, hosting a

---

[91] Old Romanian proverb: "The best kind of fish is pork."
[92] Though, if they were, I bet the negotiations would go much faster.

series of strategy sessions prior to Romania's entrance into World War I (1914–1918), when Wallachia was working to expand Greater Romania by uniting with Transylvania and Bukovina.

Despite numerous restorations[93] the inn was abandoned and decaying when I first laid eyes on it in 2007. Covered in graffiti and without a single window intact, it appeared to have been vacated only minutes after they completed the supposed restoration in the early 90s. After glacial, start-stop restoration, the inn is now open once again, serving as a hotel, restaurant, wine cellar, and pastry shop.

--------------------------------------

As for the ancillary Dracula attractions, though they could have rightly gone full-camp, for the moment Bucharest has kept it admirably subdued. However, there is one extravagant exception: Count Dracula Club.

This themed restaurant, with a side helping of haunted house, lives in a much-altered renaissance-style structure dating from 1895. There are several elaborately decorated rooms, including the "Chapel," creepily located in the basement and adorned with severed heads, chains, Dracula's coffin, and spooky music. The house is divided into several sections containing bars and dining rooms where walls drip with blood, taxidermied and mounted game heads stare down at you as you dine, and innumerable

---

[93] 1848, 1863, 1966–1970, and 1991–1992.

reproductions of engravings and paintings are scattered about. Guests are invited to wander the house or, in some cases, take a guided tour with one of the servers.

The menu borrows heavily from the *Dracula* novel with items such as "The Van Helsing Plate," "Mina's Salad," "Golden Crown Robber Steak," "Renfield's Dish" (which, if it's true to the book[94], I'd advise you to skip), and, of course, "Count Dracula's Beefsteak." You'll be relieved to hear they did not miss the opportunity for the obligatory "Death by Chocolate" dessert.

The prices are high without being extortionate and the food is surprisingly good for a themed, kitschy joint. Service and satisfied customers seem to vary depending on the night. When the restaurant is in full swing it's a cackling good time, provided you're emotionally committed to enjoying cheesy interludes during your meal. On an off night, you might find yourself drinking and dining in a lifeless if not virtually empty dining room, with the kind of unsmiling indifferent attitude that still pervades in large sections of Romania's service industry. Alas, there's an awkward and uncomfortable hard sell at the end of the night to purchase a commemorative "I Survived Dracula" certificate, which cost 10 euro at the time of writing.

If you time your visit for one of the aforementioned lively nights, "Dracula" himself will appear to play host.

---

[94] Spiders!!

Alternatively, Count Dracula Club stages theme nights on Valentine's Day and, naturally, Halloween.

------------------------------------------

After you've completed your Dracula checklist, you'll probably want to stick around for a few days, as Bucharest has the country's largest array of museums, parks, monuments, landmark buildings and, after years of needless suffering, memorable cuisine[95]. These attractions/enticements vary wildly in their ability to satisfy, but even if you just stick to the top shelf items, you could just about fill a week in the city. And that's coming from someone who has frequently gone on record as declaring Bucharest the least all-around fulfilling city in Romania.

Without going full-guidebook on you, some of the better experiences and most compelling attractions (it's important to note that these are frequently not one and the same) can be found at the Museum of the Romanian Peasant (*Muzeul Ţăranului Român*), which opened in 1906 and is located north of the city center. The museum was famously declared "European Museum of the Year" in 1996, a time when Romanian tourism, never mind Romanian museums, must have seemed like the punch line to a lazy joke. But I can testify that it is well deserved now as much as it was back then. The museum's fascinating exhibits include some

---

[95] Rather than Romania's historical eating options, which were strictly to forestall death.

90,000 pieces, hands-down the most exhaustive collection of folk art in the country, such as household items, ceramics (of which there are 18,000 items dating from the 18th century), folk costumes (20,000 pieces), furniture, carpets, photographs, wooden objects, farming equipment, textiles, tokens of rural spiritual and cultural life, and even scale models of a peasant home and a wooden church. Four more authentic wooden churches, dragged here from various locations around the country, are part of the outdoor exhibit.

In terms of civic pride, the top attraction is the National Museum of Art of Romania, housed in the Royal Palace on Revolution Square (*Piaţa Revolutiei*). Collections include both medieval and modern Romanian art, such as sculptures by Romania's beloved Constantin Brâncuşi, as well as a respectable collection of international pieces accumulated by the Romanian royal family during their relatively brief interval of power.

Out front is Revolution Square, where the Romanian Revolution went from distant skirmish in Timişoara to a pie in Ceauşescu's dumb face on December 21, 1989. In the center of the square is the 1989 Romanian Revolution memorial sculpture, called the "Memorial of Rebirth," erected in 2005. The abstract, prison shiv-shaped, marble pillar is popularly referred to as "the olive on the toothpick" (*măslina-n scobitoare*) by critics who argue that the sculpture is both silly and ill-suited for its surroundings. Some will mutter darkly that the design choice was driven by political nepotism rather than artistic merit. Also on the square is the wonderful Romanian Athenaeum concert hall and the historic, wallet-combusting Athenee Palace Hotel.

The aforementioned Palace of the Parliament[96] is a can't-miss attraction—literally. You can't miss it, because it's un-fucking-believably huge. Nicolae Ceauşescu, having had so many other megalomaniac projects die on the vine or very publicly and hilariously blow up in his face, was still bent on leaving behind a not-ridiculous, not-doomed piece of physical legacy. In a possible attempt to construct something large enough to house his ego-swollen head, plans were drawn up and work began on the Palace of the Parliament in 1980. By "work," I mean demolition to make space for this monster.

A devastating one-sixth of central Bucharest was bulldozed, including a number of historic buildings, national monuments, the Văcăreşti Monastery, the Brâncovenesc Hospital, and the National Archives. Whole neighborhoods were leveled, displacing thousands of people and, some say, causing the city's famous stray-dog problem; families who couldn't or wouldn't take their pets with them simply left them behind. It took 700 architects and 20,000 workers to build the hulking 12-story structure, which has 1,100 rooms, a 328-foot-long lobby, four labyrinth-y underground levels, and a massive nuclear bunker. To this day, it is the world's second-largest office building in surface area (the Pentagon

---

[96] A.k.a. "The People's House" (*Casa Poporului*), a.k.a. "The People's Palace."

is the largest) and the third-largest structure in volume after the Vehicle Assembly Building at the Kennedy Space Center and the Great Pyramid of Giza in Egypt.

The building is said to be constructed and furnished exclusively with Romanian materials, therefore making it a kind of nationalist showcase of the country's best artisans. While the outside is borderline cartoonish in its dictator-esque size and ornamentation, the luxurious interior is where things get downright ridiculous. Rooms and hallways are adorned with marble, oak, mosaics, gold leaf, stained-glass windows, and expensive carpets. Especially impressive are the crystal chandeliers, which are suitably enormous, some twinkling with as many as 7,000 light bulbs. The heavyweight champion of the chandeliers can be found in the Human Rights Hall (*Sala Drepturilor Omului*), weighing in at 2.5 tons[97].

Today, it houses Romania's Parliament, naturally, the Senate, the Chamber of Deputies, the Legislative Council, the Competition Council, the National Museum of Contemporary Art, the Museum, and Park of Totalitarianism and Socialist Realism, one of the largest convention centers in the world and a hodgepodge of lesser administrative offices. And yet about 30 percent of the building remains unused. Yeah, it's frickin' huge, man.

---

[97] I'd lay money on a ton of human rights being violated during the assembly and installation of that chandelier.

Nicolae Ceaușescu didn't live long enough to see the finished product[98], but you can take a guided tour to see just a few of the dazzling rooms, huge halls and quarters used by the Senate (when not in session). Historically, these tours have been led by an all-star team of Romania's most charm-deficient, least gifted English speakers, which is hard to do considering how widely English is spoken in the country. Each time I've set foot in that place, whether for a tour or just to fact-check a guidebook at the information desk, I've been pissed off by someone who viewed the maddening inconvenience of dealing with visitors as some kind of personal injustice.

After the Old Court Church, one[99] could argue that the city's next most fascinating place of worship is Stavropoleos Church (*Biserica Stavropoleos*). Built in 1724 by the Greek monk Ioanikie Stratonikeas, the tiny church's exterior is bedecked in a combination of Romanian and Byzantine architecture, the lower half bare stone and the upper half painted, including numerous spherical portraits of saints. The portico is also decorated in murals and elaborately carved Corinthian columns. Like most Romanian churches, the interior is completely covered in murals—the walls, ceiling, dome, everything. It's a cozy place, oozing with an ancient spirituality that seemingly hangs in the air—if you believe that sort of thing.

---

[98] Work wasn't completed until 1997.
[99] Me.

The adjacent courtyard is a gorgeous, green, flowery retreat, with a peristyle[100] and filled with tombstones, relics and engravings from the churches that were demolished while making space for that dazzling eyesore, the Palace of Parliament. The courtyard also happens to be one of the precious few spots in central Bucharest where the sounds of birds chirping are more prominent than the sounds of roaring traffic and honking horns.

In terms of prominent landmarks, there's The Triumphal Arch (*Arcul de Triumf*), honoring the Romanian soldiers who served in World War I, built with wood in 1922 and outfitted in its current granite form in 1936. It's plainly modeled after Paris' Arc de Triomphe, decorated with sculptures by several Romanian artists, and was one of the key elements added to Calea Victoriei as part of its Champs-Élysées-ification. It stands 85 feet high and has an interior staircase leading to a viewing platform where some fine panoramic photos can be taken.

Briefly, some of Bucharest's mid-range attractions include the National History Museum, the National Museum of Contemporary Art (sharing space in the Royal Palace with the National Museum of Art), Museum of Natural History, and the Eastern European standby, a Military Museum.

---

[100] Columned porch surrounding a courtyard.

# I'mma Get Medieval on Yo' Ass

With the work in Bucharest completed, Dracula now had three near-impenetrable fortresses from which to stage attacks and to use as retreats, in addition to legions of highly trained and well-paid mercenaries complementing forces drafted from his motivated subjects. Just in the nick of time, too.

In 1459, while Dracula busied himself with croaking decades' worth of family foes and preparing for the Ottoman reckoning, in far-off Rome Pope Pius II was also growing concerned with the Ottomans tearing up the Balkans. He raised a bunch of cash and put out the call for Europe to get its shit together and organize a crusade against the Ottomans before they grew strong enough to drive all the way to the Atlantic.

Alas, once again, pretty much all the major European players at the time declined to help. Many were embroiled in civil war[101], drawn-out border skirmishes with neighbors[102], just happy to be rid of previous conquerors and didn't give a shit about hijinks happening so far away[103], planning their own expansion[104], and the always-tempting allure of

---

[101] England.

[102] England and France.

[103] Spain, still swooning over finally ridding themselves of the Moors.

[104] Portugal, who was planning to circumnavigate Africa, maneuvering itself into the Far East and, eventually, having a hand in sending an asshole called Columbus on a half-baked westerly voyage to Asia that washed up in the New World.

amassing riches and political power as quickly as possible[105].
Holy Roman Emperor Frederick III again pledged help and
then, on the advice of his astrologers, focused instead on his
ongoing scheme to unseat the ambitious and covetous King
Matthias Corvinus in Hungary, son of our old pal John
Hunyadi[106].

Oddly, while those in Europe who were square in the
Sultan's crosshairs dithered and made excuses, help came
from a hodgepodge of places in the east, including firm
promises of troops from Armenia, Georgia, Mingrelia[107],
Karaman in Asia Minor and Iran from none other than
Sultan Mehmed's brother-in-law Uzun Hazan[108]. With this
newfound well of support, Pope Pius envisioned squeezing
the Ottomans on their eastern and western fronts
simultaneously, though he still didn't hold out much hope
for a serious threat to come from the indifferent west.
Nonetheless, he raised a bunch of cash and started putting
plans into motion.

---

[105] Large parts of Italy, including the Medicis. Venice had started to
break a sweat over the advancing Ottomans, but stalled for time by
trying to reach a diplomatic solution. By the time Venice joined the
battle against the Turks in 1464, Dracula was already defeated and facing
a long, involuntary stay in Buda.
[106] After Hunyadi's death, and being briefly thrown in prison with his
brother Ladislaus by King Ladislaus V of Hungary, Matthias was set free
and elected king during the rebellion after King Ladislaus over-played
his hand and had Ladislaus Hunyadi killed in prison. Matthias ruled
from 1458 to 1490. (Did you follow that? Yeah, there were one too many
dudes named "Ladislaus" at the time.)
[107] Located on the eastern shores of the Black Sea.
[108] Even Mehmed's own family wished the prick ill.

Vlad Dracula, by now thoroughly sick of distant Ottoman oppression of Wallachia, was the only leader in Christian Europe to answer the Pope's call[109]. Though some sources say that Matthias Corvinus also joined the effort to chase the Ottomans back to Constantinople, it appears he too hung back, or gave up very quickly, in the hopes that someone else would step up and defend his eastern frontier for him.

Dracula's first act of defiance against the Sultan was to withhold payment of that galling "tax" and the able-bodied men Wallachia was still contributing to the Sultan's military each year. When Ottoman envoys arrived to persuade Vlad to cough up the overdue payment, Vlad feigned disproportionate indignance when they failed to respectfully raise their "hats" to him, meaning their turbans, giving him the engineered excuse to kill them by nailing their turbans to their heads.

When news of this atrocity reached Mehmed in Constantinople, he vowed to get serious with the uppity Prince. Mehmed had already made a name for himself as an ambitious, decadent, brutal ruler[110], immediately unpopular with his subjects, with undisguised plans for aggressive land-grabbing. Yet he still had command of an enormous, seemingly inexhaustible army, probably triple the size

---

[109] Like he had any choice, sitting there in Wallachia, which would one way or another be a crusade battleground, but still...

[110] Mehmed, wanting to eliminate even the slightest hint of future rivalry, had his half-brother, only a tiny child at the time, drowned in a bathtub.

necessary to slap Dracula and Wallachia into line once and for all.

While Mehmed busied himself with vengeance logistics, Dracula was still tidying his realm of his own potential usurpers. After tracking down and finally offing Dan III, he went on the hunt for his own half-brother, Vlad the Monk. Vlad the Monk had a brief ground-swell of boyar support in Sibiu to take the throne in Wallachia, before being scared into hiding by the rapidly accumulating tales of Vlad's testicle-shrinking atrocities. Nonetheless, Dracula knew he couldn't let the monk lie low and wait for an opportune time to strike, so the chase was on. Though Vlad once again rained terror across Transylvania while searching for his half-brother, he was unsuccessful in flushing him out[111].

Having grown tired of the seesaw fighting and understandably preoccupied by Ottoman activity south of the Danube, both Dracula and King Matthias managed to broker several peace deals with cities across Transylvania— deals that included support for Dracula's impending confrontation with the Turks and Dracula grudgingly paying reparations for all the death and destruction he'd previously inflicted on Braşov. With his west and north sides now firmly secured, Dracula could throw all his weight against the encroaching Ottomans.

---

[111] Vlad the Monk would go on to eventually rule Wallachia in 1481 and 1482-1495.

Meanwhile, Sultan Mehmed had already started campaigning against what remained of the free Balkan states, including easily rolling over Semendria, Serbia's last bastion of independence. Other territories, knees knocking, simply signed whatever peace treaty the Sultan offered (effectively surrendering). During the escalation, Mihály Szilágy, Dracula's longtime ally and brother-caliber close friend, was captured by the Ottomans and tortured to death while being interrogated for details about the West's military plans and preparedness. Dracula's anger, already itching to poke holes in some Ottoman torsos, went nuclear.

With Mehmed already battling daunting forces coming at him from the east and Dracula needing time to get his troops ready, both men were simultaneously and independently trying to buy themselves time. This predicament worked out in Vlad's favor. Mehmed made an apparent, though probably insincere, last ditch-attempt to mend fences. Dracula agreed, and an Ottoman envoy was sent to meet Dracula at Giurgiu fortress in Wallachia in November 1461. In what must have been a dizzying flurry of intercepted communications and spy work, Mehmed learned Dracula was definitely in cahoots with Hungary and instead planned to have Dracula captured at Giurgiu and dragged back to Constantinople behind an incontinent donkey[112]. Not long after, Dracula learned of Mehmed's extraction plan. He and his crew geared up and succeeded in capturing the

---

[112] Probably.

Sultan's envoys, some one thousand troops in total, marching them to Târgovişte and, naturally, impaling every one of them outside the palace.

With that overt rebellion out in the open, Dracula went on to recapture the fortress at Giurgiu, famously disguising himself as an Ottoman soldier and using his Turkish fluency to convince some dim-witted commander to open the gates. Vlad's men charged in and wiped them out, which must have been a nice bit of cathartic justice, being that Dracula's own father had built the fortress and the Ottomans had captured and controlled it since way back in 1447. Dracula, apparently not the sentimental type, looted and burned the fortress down.

By that stage, Mehmed was likely fantasizing about de-boning Dracula alive, but he was still battling for all his worth in the east and was thus unable to send the requisite forces to delete Vlad from existence.

With the Ottomans on their heels, and knowing a toe-to-toe battle with Ottoman forces was doomed to fail, Dracula's forces sidled into Bulgaria in the winter of 1461-1462 to launch a series of daring surprise attacks on unsuspecting advance teams of Turkish troops staging themselves for war with Wallachia. Over the course of an epic two-week rampage, Dracula and his men covered an astounding 800 kilometers, west to east along the Danube, all the way to the Danube Delta, during which time his forces tirelessly impaled some 23,000 Turks—and also an unlucky bunch of Bulgarians who were in the wrong place at the wrong time. Yet more uncounted troops were killed by burning down houses being used as refuge and still others in hasty fashion when there wasn't enough time for a proper, methodical impaling. Dracula's forces also destroyed every town on the Bulgarian side of the Danube that the Ottomans might use to stage a river crossing for attacks in Wallachia. For the first time since his grandfather Mircea's reign, Wallachia enjoyed complete control of the Danube.

A proud Dracula sent a highly satisfied letter to King Matthias with an amazingly detailed account of how many people he'd impaled at each stop in his campaign. As a thoughtful "bonus," Dracula also sent Matthias two giant sacks filled with a trail-mix of severed noses, ears and heads.

Mehmed, still embroiled in both defending himself against armies coming from Asia Minor and trying to lock down Corinth in Greece, once again sent a relatively insubstantial force, 18,000 men, to take a swing at Vlad by razing the important port city of Brălia. This effort was successful, but the emboldened commander of this army went off the rails, exceeding his mandate and laying waste to Wallachian villages inland. Dracula and his forces raced to the area, caught the Ottomans from behind as they were heading back to Brălia, and slaughtered some 10,000 of them.

By now, Dracula's numerous bite-sized exploits were starting to have a noticeable impact on the overall strength of the Ottoman army. Word of this almost unbelievable success against seemingly overwhelming forces had spread across Transylvania, Hungary, Italy, and even to Western Europe. Not only was Dracula keeping the Ottomans too discombobulated to launch the long-feared invasion into Christian Europe, but he was actually *pushing them back* toward Constantinople as they closed ranks.

The moniker "Sir Impaler" was being anxiously whispered in senior Ottoman military circles and some officials were so utterly freaked out over the idea of facing Dracula in battle that they talked of abandoning their posts and fleeing somewhere, anywhere, into Asia Minor and— why not?—buying that sailboat they'd always dreamed of.

Pope Pius, already a bit smitten with Dracula, despite his apparent inexhaustible rage and thirst for gruesome killing, was jubilant upon hearing this news, being that months earlier he'd had little hope of anything more than negligible progress against the Ottomans from the west.

An infuriated Sultan Mehmed abandoned the siege at Corinth[113], quickly wrapped up a few other campaigns in Asia, and then began amassing a shock-and-awe army that he would personally lead against Vlad. Though numbers vary wildly depending on the source, prevailing logic suggests the Ottoman forces that headed for Wallachia in May 1462 totaled 60,000 highly skilled Ottoman troops, archers, warriors, and body guards, including their celebrated artillery force of 120 cannons, still swaggering from having busted through Constantinople's legendary

---

[113] I wonder if Dracula ever got a thank you note from the Corinthians?

defenses. Additionally, some 30,000 irregulars were drafted from conquered Turkish territories, closely monitored by overseers who essentially functioned as slave drivers, whipping or killing anyone showing signs of slowing down or fleeing. Altogether, this legion was dazzlingly large, fortified by ironmongers, tailors, wheel makers, cobblers, cooks, historians[114], "entertainers[115]," horses, buffalo, bison and camels. Finally, brought along for the ride, and presumably to plop his handsome butt on the throne at the conclusion of Wallachia's annihilation, was Dracula's estranged brother, Radu.

In contrast, it's estimated that Dracula had only about 30,000 bodies in his army. Dracula's forces included fierce fighters, an assortment of paid mercenaries from across Europe, and peasant troops so fiercely loyal that it's said their steadfast silence, even under excruciating interrogation, gave appreciative pause to Mehmed himself. Though to say that Dracula had a legitimate force of 30,000 is a bit deceptive. His army also included all the women and children over the age of 12 that he could round up and arm with a weapon[116].

Crazy as Dracula sometimes sounds, he was not devoid of practicality. He didn't have any doubt that his forces would be quickly flattened by an Ottoman invasion of

---

[114] To carefully document their great victories.

[115] Women to make sure the men were taken care of, if you catch my drift.

[116] Naturally, the wealthiest families avoided military service by hiding in the mountains or disappearing into Transylvania.

that size and once again asked neighboring Christian states for military support[117]. With momentum on his side and the support of a determined pope, he hoped to appeal to leaders who could help defend Christian Europe's doorstep, lest it be overtaken, followed quickly by Europe's foyer, sitting room, kitchen, pantry and so forth.

Yet again, no one answered the call to come to Wallachia's aid, not even that ass-wipe and supposed ally King Matthias, who chose instead the highly shortsighted option of standing at the ready should King Frederick decide to head-fake in his direction.[118]

Though his previous flurry of small-scale, surprise attacks had been exceedingly effective, Dracula knew such tactics against a colossal force of 90,000 troops was unlikely to bring total victory. But, for lack of any other option or aid, Vlad continued launching his raids, making life hell for Mehmed and his men.

In a bit of good luck, the Ottomans' advance was actually hindered by their prized cannons. Only slightly more portable than square boulders on the busted roads, thick forests and goopy marshes of Bulgaria and Wallachia, their mighty artillery became crippling liabilities.

---

[117] It's said that with one of these letters he sent along a "gift," similar to the one he'd sent King Matthias, as a sign of his resolve to cut down any Turks who tried to march through Wallachia. It contained 23,883 severed noses, carved off the faces of his enemies.

[118] Though he was too dead to witness the ramifications himself, Matthias' lack of support probably contributed to Hungary's being conquered by the Ottomans 64 years later in 1526, which included the murder of his successor Louis II.

Dracula was able to keep close tabs on the speed and position of the Ottoman force once they entered his territory. Not only did his scouts know the terrain intimately, but they had eyes and ears literally everywhere in the form of villagers and farmers who monitored the troops as they struggled past and then duly reported their progress to the scouts.

Crossing the Danube was perhaps the most difficult obstacle for Mehmed's forces. The Ottoman fleet of 150 ships was rendered all but useless in the campaign after Vlad had destroyed all useable ports while conquering the Danube the previous year. Their contribution was limited to attacking the fortresses at Brălia and Chilia[119]. Attempts to cross the river all failed under a hail of Wallachian arrows.

With extreme effort and several hundred lost troops, the Ottomans were eventually able to creep across the Danube at night using fishermen's barges, marking a turning point in Dracula's strategy.

Though still bounding out of bushes and whacking isolated, straggling pockets of Turks whenever possible, Vlad's forces were now effectively in retreat, heading for Târgovişte. Even in retreat, the Wallachians made life extravagantly miserable for the Ottomans. They ruthlessly poisoned water supplies, burned forests, herded farm animals that might be slaughtered for food up into the mountains, created marsh obstacles by diverting small

---

[119] And later evacuating retreating troops.

rivers, and set booby traps like camouflaged pits big enough to swallow an ox.

The Wallachians got another break in that the summer of 1462 was the hottest on record. Thus, the Ottomans stumbled along baking in their armor for days at a time without the benefit of shelter, fresh water, or even shade for extended periods. In addition to this torment, Dracula's forces would periodically gallop out of unlikely side roads, kill everyone in sight, then retreat before the woozy, heat-stroking Ottomans could muster a serious counterattack.

Ever imaginatively cruel, Dracula gathered those suffering from leprosy, tuberculosis, syphilis and, most effectively, the bubonic plague, dressed them in Turkish outfits and sent them to mingle with and infect the Turks[120].

This unrelenting torment and lack of food and water soon reduced Mehmed's forces to a shell of their former might. Mehmed, himself a noted master of psychological warfare and shockingly vicious, was beyond exasperation, bordering on traumatized, by the scale and relentlessness of Dracula's brutality. Confidence rapidly evaporating and conquering spirits snuffed, the beleaguered Turks nonetheless staggered on, moving ever closer to Vlad's throne at Târgovişte's Princely Court.

---

[120] This tactic was said to be one of the earliest known implementations of germ warfare.

But the crescendo of Vlad's guerrilla tactics and psychological warfare was yet to come. During one final surge, Dracula staged the so-called "Night Attack" in June of 1462 a few hours after sunset near Târgovişte in the Carpathian foothills. Wallachian forces took out a staggering 15,000 Turks, while suffering the loss of 5,000 troops over the course of a few presumably chaotic hours. Dracula, right up at the front of the fighting, very nearly succeeded in a daring assassination attempt on Mehmed himself. Though he'd personally done reconnaissance on the camp while in disguise, in the darkness and confusion Vlad attacked the wrong tent and Mehmed escaped.

The surviving Ottomans limped on to Târgovişte. Sixty miles short of the city, whatever resolve they had left was squashed into oblivion by one final act of mind-bending horror. Dracula's men had erected a "forest" of 20,000 staked and gutted Turks collected from Vlad's previous raids, neatly arranged in an enormous fence-like semicircle. Some of the corpses had been there for months, exposed to the elements and pecking birds, and in the heat of the summer the stench of death must have been nauseating.

Mehmed paused, presumably barfed in his mouth a little, and said something to the effect of "fuck this," before turning around and retreating to Constantinople. Even in retreat, Dracula's cloud of death followed Mehmed, as the plague he'd seeded in the Ottoman army spread out of control and took even more lives without a single arrow having been fired.

Any savoring of triumph by Dracula was brief. In a totally unexpected move, his own cousin, Stephen of Moldavia, formerly his closest ally, turned on him. Commanding an army that included Turkish reinforcements, who apparently didn't have anything better to do, Stephen attacked the fortress at Chilia. He failed, a joint Wallachian-Hungarian force killed many more Turks, and Stephen himself suffered a leg wound that never fully healed for the remainder of his life.

Stephen's betrayal wasn't personal[121], but an act of self-preservation for Moldavia. If Dracula failed in his war with the Turks, which any betting man with any sense would naturally assume, Stephen wanted to ensure that Moldavia wouldn't be conquered next by preemptively aligning himself with the Turks. Also, the fact that Hungarians were at Chilia was an added incentive as Stephen was still seething about Matthias Corvinus harboring Petru Aaron, the man who had killed his father.

Back in Târgovişte, Radu had been left behind with some of the Sultan's rattled minions as the Turks retreated. With Dracula off tormenting the retreating Ottomans, Radu began to erode his brother's power in the capital via diplomatic avenues. With the help of friendly boyars and his beguiling charm, Radu went to work persuading the Wallachians to accept him as their prince. It turns out Radu wasn't just a pretty face. With a previously unknown

---

[121] Though one assumes Dracula did not interpret it that way.

cunning, he turned his powers of persuasion up to '11' and succeeded in selling himself as a kinder, gentler prince. Having not a trace of impaling instinct or, more importantly, proclivities for random, murderous violence against his own people was a strong selling point, by that stage. With Wallachia's independence secured and the populace exhausted and beaten from all the military action, Radu must have looked like the last piece to their salvation and, with a new, favorable agreement with the Ottomans, the swiftest, least painful return to business as usual.

Even as Dracula was still stabbing and disemboweling for his kingdom, handily winning one last skirmish against the Turks in Buzău, his army of peasants and volunteers was already quietly deserting their posts and scurrying to Radu's protection. Soon his forces were reduced to just his bodyguards and the remainder of his hired mercenaries. Dracula knew he needed to close ranks, regroup and wait for reinforcements that, he deeply hoped, Matthias was dispatching to Transylvania at a full gallop. And what better place to lie low than his mountaintop fortress Poenari Citadel?

------------------------------

Having rallied after washing out their underwear and listening to Radu deliver what must have been the most effective pep talk of all time, the remaining Ottomans pursued Vlad to Poenari. After the surely grueling task of hauling their light artillery up to Poenari, their bombardments barely scratched the castle's thick walls.

Insane as it sounded, Radu had no choice but to order a full assault on the perilously steep mountain and its seemingly impregnable fortress. The people hunkered down inside were probably confident about preventing troops from breaching the walls, but there was the matter of outlasting a prolonged siege in Poenari's relatively confined walls, which would surely end in their starvation. But it never got to that point.

As you may have gathered by now, Vlad was not a people person. Despite his newfound fame as valiant defender of Wallachia and Ottoman scourge, the boyars in the area had all jumped on the Radu bandwagon. Radu's angelic good looks and even temperament aside, the boyars were likely still unhappy about Dracula's alienating them, undermining their authority and, of course, slaughtering and enslaving them in droves. So, Dracula had lost virtually all his support in Wallachia and there was still no word or indication that Matthias had sent Hungarian troops to help him. In short, Dracula was screwed, but, being cut off from all communication, he hadn't quite realized it yet.

In what must have been Dracula's umpteenth nine-lives-caliber, narrow escape, a Romanian-born member of the Ottoman janissary corps, apparently still quietly clinging to some nationalistic pride, managed to get a warning message to Dracula by attaching it to an arrow that he impressively shot into one of the castle's tiny windows on a moonless, pitch-black night. Fully apprised of their abandoned, dire situation, the fortress burst into activity.

Before a rational plan could be formed, Vlad's wife[122], Jusztina Szilagyi of Moldavia, declared she'd rather be fish food than be captured by the Turks and immediately flung herself from the towers of Poenari into the Argeş River valley. Legend has it the river turned red with her blood and to this day that section of the Argeş is called "The Lady's River." Dracula didn't have the luxury of mourning; he needed an escape plan.

Tiptoeing away from a mountaintop stronghold completely surrounded by legions of soldiers aching to fillet you like a carp is about as tricky as it sounds. Legend has it that Vlad was able to escape Poenari with the help of the aforementioned local clan called the Dobrins, who lived in (what is today known as) the village of Arefu in the valley below. It's said Dracula descended down the aforementioned secret shaft inside the castle that led to a cave and then to the river. Once there, Vlad met the Dobrins, who quietly escorted him out of harm's way on horses whose shoes had been nailed on backwards, making it appear as though they had been walking *toward* the castle[123].

Vlad took refuge in one of John Hunyadi's old fortresses on the summit of the Făgăraş mountain range, in sight of Braşov. Having received word that Matthias was finally on his way, he decided to hole up in the small fortress and wait for his ally to race to his rescue.

---

[122] Or concubine, depending on who's telling the story.
[123] Apparently, outwitting people in the 15th century wasn't especially challenging.

# Bran Castle

That asshat Matthias Corvinus virtually crawled to his supposed ally's assistance. Even by 15th-century standards, Matthias couldn't have possibly moved more slowly in the direction of Braşov. This meandering journey included a *month-long stop* in Sibiu to discuss diplomatic and/or military action that, if he ever got there, would be launched from Braşov.

Matthias' slow pace did not go unnoticed by the pope and others in the West who were still financially supporting him for the promised crusade. Despite his plainly obvious dawdling, Matthias was somehow able to keep relations breezy with his benefactors through the help of several supposedly independent reports of his diligent progress. Meanwhile, the window of opportunity to launch a punishing and definitive offensive on the dazed Ottomans was slipping away.

Once Matthias finally wandered into Braşov, Dracula immediately joined him[124] for five strained weeks of negotiations. Despite Dracula's heroics still being regarded with awe and admiration across Europe, the unpredictable (read: asshole) tendencies he'd displayed at home had lost him his throne and the loyalty of his citizens. By this stage,

---

[124] It was, incidentally, the first time the two had met as adults. Matthias had evidently not matured gracefully. He was described as being a "diminutive, bullish figure" with a "high forehead, and deep-set but shifty eyes." It appears few people, leaders at any rate, were particularly pleasing to the eye in the era.

he was little more than a refugee hiding in Transylvania who happened to have a respectably dangerous gang of thugs at his command.

Someone who had fallen to such a position of weakness in that era wouldn't usually warrant even a postcard from someone in Matthias' position, but by now Matthias had happily received enormous sums of money[125] to organize a crusade, thus he was forced to meet with Dracula to maintain the appearance of progress. Matthias cautiously kept up the façade of planning to unseat the Ottoman-friendly Radu in Wallachia, then charge in pursuit of the discombobulated Ottomans, which everyone agreed was best accomplished with the assistance of his theoretical ally—the highly motivated, extremely talented Impaler.

In fact, Radu, who was turning out to be a far more brilliant political strategist than anyone had given him credit for, had not only locked down Wallachia, but had also persuaded the leaders of the pivotal Transylvanian cities of Sibiu and Braşov to recognize him as prince. Envoys from these two cities had subsequently motioned Matthias aside during his strategy meetings with Vlad and persuaded him to also support Radu. In one of his Top 5 of All Time disastrous life decisions, Matthias also secretly signed a five-year truce with the Ottomans—precisely the opposite of what

---

[125] Matthias' wealth had evaporated due to costly political and military maneuvering at home and stringing the pope along seems to have been his extremely shortsighted, temporary solution to that problem.

he'd earnestly agreed to do with his ill-gotten crusading allowance.

It's also theorized that Matthias' multifaceted, harebrained betrayal may have been egged on by his trusted astrologer, who was being quietly bankrolled by German interests. Those Germans were still pissed off at Dracula for tormenting their Saxon brothers and had a calculated long game to shut him down, permanently.

Above all else, Matthias' main motivation was to finally get his shot at the title of Emperor back home. Frederick III was being besieged by his own people in Vienna over ambitious tax increases, finally opening the door for Matthias to position himself as first in line to snatch the crown when the shit hit the fan. By comparison, the wearisome antics of the Turks, and their distant rabblerousing in the Balkans, didn't warrant Matthias' time and resources. After all, there was a freshly inked truce, and anyway they hardly seemed a threat while composing themselves after the physical and mental pounding they had taken from Dracula. Furthermore, they had lately busied themselves with the escalating fighting in the east with Anatolia. Matthias was thus comfortable letting the Turks stew on the back burner for a while.

Dracula, stuck in perhaps the weakest position he'd been in since fleeing the Ottoman court, wasn't in any shape to demand much. Additionally, with his usual network of informers no longer feeding him intel, he had no way of knowing he was about to get punk'd.

While no doubt fighting back a conniving smirk, Matthias sent Dracula and his crew off with a supporting contingent of his men under orders to handle the Radu situation. He promised to personally lead a much larger, trailing force that would then join with Dracula to finally go gallivanting off for the long-promised crusade. Instead, Matthias' men succeeded in separating Dracula from the remainder of his loyal mercenaries, arrested him without a fuss, and hauled him to Buda in time for Christmas 1462. His second term as prince had ended.

According to some sources, Matthias' guys, probably feeling exceptionally pleased about leashing the illustrious Vlad Dracula, stopped at Bran Castle on the way to Buda and threw their captive in the dungeon while they indulged in some R&R.

Maybe.

--------------------------------

To this day, there is confusion about when or if Dracula ever set foot in Bran Castle. So much research has been done and so much speculation has been speculated that even highly reliable sources differ wildly. During the four or five trips I made to Bran to update Lonely Planet guidebooks, it seemed each visit I would inevitably stumble upon new compelling evidence that threw into question the content of my previous update[126]. So, I hit the research especially hard for this chapter to find the facts—or at least what appears to be my

---

[126] Sorry, Lonely Planet editors!

best guess at facts. But first let's discuss Bran Castle itself, because it's right up there with the best man-made attractions in all of Romania.

Work on the castle began in 1378 by Saxons from nearby Braşov who wanted to defend the Bran pass against the ever-present threat of steamrolling by the Turks. Its original iteration was operational by 1382 and, after centuries of additions and expansions by successive residents, including Teutonic Knights, Hungarian kings, and finally Romanian royalty, it became the fairytale, multi-turreted, aesthetically vampire-worthy structure we know today. It veritably oozes mystical energy, seemingly growing organically out of the rocky fastness that serves as its base and harmoniously forming into castle. Arriving invaders' testicles must have retreated into their abdomens upon first glimpsing the high-set, hulking, nearly 200-foot tall castle, backed by twin, foreboding mountains and looking utterly the part of a full-blown, dark magic wizard lair.

Unsurprisingly, this is one of Romania's top sights and tourist trap bait of the first order, receiving some 560,000 visitors each year, according to a recent article in *The Telegraph*. To access the castle you must park in one of the massive parking lots in the valley below, wind your way through a sea of tour buses, run the gauntlet through the tatty "market," filled with cheap souvenirs and shouting touts, elbow and gasp your way up the hill, and finally wait your turn to pass through the bottleneck entrance. I make it sound horrible, but believe me it's worth it.

After viewing the dazzling exterior from every angle, the interior has been known to disappoint some. It was renovated and updated in the 1920s when Queen Marie, daughter to England's Queen Victoria, moved in and other royals started using it as a summer retreat. When Marie died in 1938 her daughter Princess Ileana took the keys, briefly opening up the castle in 1944 as a hospital for WWII soldiers. The communists were standing at the ready to take control of Bran when King Michael and the royal family were bounced into exile with 24 hours' notice in 1948.

After a troublingly lengthy period of indecision, during which time you might imagine Bran was being considered for use as a swanky, communist elite party house, Bran was opened to the public as a museum in 1957.

The decorative finishes are largely 19th-century hunting-lodge chic and room after room is filled with elaborately carved wooden tables, chairs, vanities, chests, and dressers imported from Western Europe by Queen Marie, along with a few older museum-worthy pieces. In-wall display cases hold ceramic art and aging books. Sitting rooms are bedecked with large fireplaces, throne-like chairs, and bearskin rugs, heads still attached, natch. A sturdy, wooden canopy bed with bible stories ornately carved into the head and footboards is the hands-down highlight of the furnishings. Whether or not the wretched excess of the 19th-century furnishings and décor impress you, wandering the seemingly endless rooms, balconies, claustrophobic stairways, nooks and crannies will appeal to your inner child. (If you're not dead inside.)

The inner courtyard, which is ringed by multi-level balconies—some stacked five high—proves how massive the castle truly is. Though I've never seen it myself, the fountain in the center of the courtyard is alleged to hide the entrance to a labyrinth of underground passages.

To its credit, though pretty much everyone in the market down the hill works the Count Dracula angle for everything it's worth, the interior of the castle doesn't have a hint of vampire-themed paraphernalia.

Guided tours of the castle's interior seem to run at random, but if you stumble into one, it's worthwhile. At the foot of the castle and near the souvenir market is an open-air village museum with roughly a dozen traditional buildings. The same ticket for the castle affords you entrance to the museum.

Down the hill in the town of Bran is the nine-room Vama Bran Museum, which contains some of the relics you were probably hoping to see inside the castle, including ancient plates, furniture, and various sundries.

In 2005, Romania belatedly began the process of returning property grabbed by the communists in the 1940s and '50s to its rightful owners, including Bran Castle, which was awarded to Dominic von Habsburg, an architect living in New York and the son and heir of Princess Ileana. After some stutter steps, including Romania's parliament having second thoughts and briefly trying to take the castle back, citing misinterpretation of national property law and succession, Habsburg took ownership and promptly put the castle on the market for a reported $135 million (USD). After a good deal of breath-holding, he took it off the market and, to everyone's relief, reopened it as a private museum in June 2009.

In May 2014 the aging Hapsburgs, by then in their 70s, decided that maintaining the ancient structure, beset with plumbing problems and a worrying bathroom deficiency, was perhaps better suited for younger people. After offering to sell the castle for $80 million to the Romanian government, who declined, Dominic invited offers for the property. But not just anyone could bid. "If someone comes in with a reasonable offer, we will look at who they are, what they are proposing, and will seriously entertain the idea," said a representative. This presumably means someone who intends to preserve the castle in its current condition and keep it open as a tourist sight rather than turn it into a Goth nightclub or Count Dracula-themed haunted house. Dominic has cantankerously stated that the incessant Dracula/vampire associations with Bran are "not OK."

Details are vague, but the Hapsburgs allegedly see Bran someday becoming a destination, like where people spend the night, both inside the castle and also possibly on a nearby parcel of land large enough to build a small hotel. One hopes this arrangement would still allow for tourist visiting hours. As beset with crowds and frustrating as Bran can sometimes be, it would be a massive blow to Romanian tourism to lose this outstanding attraction.

---------------------------------------

Now what about Bran Castle's muddy association with Vlad Dracula? One plausible theory (kinda) is that Vlad hunkered down in Bran Castle in 1462 for a few nights on his way north, after slithering away from the Ottoman besieged Poenari Citadel. This is mere speculation on my part, but one wonders why the Saxons controlling the castle at the time didn't succumb to the tempting opportunity for swift vengeance against Dracula. If you recall, Vlad had recently sacked Braşov and impaled the living scat out of a good portion of its social elite. It must have taken heroic willpower to not hog-tie his ass, strap him to a donkey with mange, shove it in the direction of the nearest Ottoman horde, and then party like it was 1499.

I'm guessing they resisted this urge due to the unifying panic attack the region was experiencing at the possibility of Turkish annihilation. Drac was, after all, one of the precious few individuals in Europe who was not only wily and crazy enough to go on the offensive against the overwhelming Ottoman forces, but was actually *succeeding* in slowing the Turks down, all while putting the fear of God into them in the process. So, in the interest of not becoming yet another whipped and owned Ottoman outpost, the Saxons must have decided to suck it up and help the fleeing Vlad.

Or did they? There's an oft-repeated story of Vlad being imprisoned here for a couple of months in 1462. Perhaps the Saxons *did* lock up him up for the Braşov indignity, only later calming down and letting him off the chain to go wreak more Ottoman damage.

What seems most likely is the theory I floated at the beginning of this chapter: Dracula was temporarily locked up at Bran Castle several months later, after he was betrayed and captured by Matthias Corvinus' men.

Of course, it's possible that both incidents happened. Researching 15th-century events that transpired in the wilds of Transylvania, especially those recorded based on biased testimonies and hearsay, is hard. Let's just leave it at that.

-----------------------------------------

A castle as prominent and lavish as Bran naturally attracted a frontier settlement to form around it, one composed of traders and merchants doing business with the castle as well as housing for the castle's support staff. Today Bran is a modest town of 5,600, many of whom are still involved with the castle, either as staff or working in the hospitality industry for the area's hotels and restaurants.

Despite being largely a tourism-oriented town just steps away from one of the most popular sights in Romania, it's extremely low-key, green and lovely, sitting on the photogenic spot where plains meet the Bucegi and Piatra Craiului mountain ranges. Tiny pensions, villas and private homes leasing rooms account for much of the town, while eating options are, when last I checked, pretty basic—mainly pizza joints and a few places serving OK Romanian food designed for those seeking a quick, forgettable lunch.

Bran has likely avoided going full Orlando because there isn't much to see or do aside from the castle. As such the vast majority of visitors don't spend the night here, instead choosing to sleep in the livelier environs of Braşov, a mere 30 kilometers (18.5 miles) to the northeast. A squillion mini-buses zap between the two cities every day, also allowing for a hop-off/hop-on stop at the previously described Râşnov Fortress, roughly half way between Bran and Braşov.

Bran gets it fair share of overnighters, though, with its modest business and meeting facilities driven by a hilltop, resort-like, 12-building complex with line-of-sight views of the castle, three restaurants, three pools, a zip line, an indoor basketball court, playhouse, and a "petting zoo" composed of two deer.

Bran also gets a dash of adventure travelers, many of them arriving exhausted and in dire need of a shower after staggering down Bucegi's demanding hiking trails. These trails are almost exclusively one-way from the peak of Bucegi down to Bran. Only lunatics start in Bran and hike up that monster.

Hikers start in Buşteni, take a cable car up the mountain to Babele, and start hiking northwest to Bran from there. If you fancy yourself a hiking badass, it's possible to reach Bran in one day, assuming a very early start. People who move slower or simply want to pause frequently to take in the spectacular scenery and sheer drops into valleys on either side of the trail should allot two days and either camp somewhere or spend a night at Cabana Omu.

The trail from Omu down to Bran Castle is strenuous and evil, dropping some 2,000 meters (6,560 feet) down through the tree line, then into thick forest, and finally along a logging road (read: lengthy mud pit) leading to Bran. This segment alone is a good five hours of steeply inclined, slippery hell. Trying to do it in reverse, I'd say allow for 15 hours, 15-27 minor injuries and a sprained something. Seriously, don't go this way.

# The Third Act

With visions of emperoring dancing through his head and the unruly Vlad Dracula literally tied up, if Matthias Corvinus celebrated at all, it was quickly interrupted by a political and PR record-scratch sound effect.

Matthias' long-promised crusade was clearly not happening and grumbles of displeasure were floating in from European leaders, folks who were likely sitting with buckets of popcorn and impatiently waiting for a rousing reenactment of the Ottomans being crushed. Rome and Venice were particularly displeased, demanding a detailed report about how, exactly, their crusading funds were being spent. Furthermore, people across Europe had barely sobered up from toasting Dracula's unbelievable victory against the Turks; now Matthias had thrown him in the dungeon of Buda Castle? Matthias had some 'splainin' to do.

In lieu of any legitimate justification, Matthias made his case with three letters that had suddenly materialized, supposedly from Dracula's own hand[127]. The letters, written in a decidedly un-Dracula-like friendly and familiar tone, were allegedly sent to Mehmed, Stephen of Moldavia, and an Ottoman ally. They openly indicated that Dracula, after slaughtering tens of thousands of Turks, had experienced an electroshock-therapy-caliber change in attitude and intended to help the Ottomans roll over Transylvania and

---

[127] Though, curiously, only copies could be produced as evidence.

Hungary, including plans to capture Matthias himself. Using these dubious documents as fuel, Matthias' PR team back in Hungary went to work fanning the flames of this character assassination, depicting Dracula as pure evil, rather than only slightly more depraved than average for the era, and making the case that he needed to be executed for his countless atrocities and betrayal of Christian Europe.

The validity of these letters, uncharacteristically subservient in tone, poorly composed, sent from an unknown place in Transylvania called "Rothal" [128] and, of course, not even in Dracula's hand, should have been considered dubious by anyone who had ever met Dracula[129]. And for some time, they most certainly were.

The senate in Venice was particularly skeptical and, after receiving several brief and vague explanations about the situation from Buda, made repeated attempts to uncover the precise circumstances of Dracula's arrest.

In Rome, Pope Pius was also in a fit of bewilderment and deep suspicion over his boy Vlad switching teams suddenly and without explanation after years of well-documented resentment and later slaughtering of the Ottomans. European leaders and diplomats across the board couldn't comprehend this turn of events and some even made thinly veiled proclamations that Matthias had

---

[128] Eventually revealed to be fictitious.
[129] It's now believed these letters were written by a chaplain in Braşov, a man who was among the countless people irreversibly aggrieved by Dracula's previous violence and destruction in his city.

engineered a fallacy and may have even been in cahoots with Mehmed, which of course was precisely the case.

It seems Matthias was able to spin these accusations and probes for some time. Meanwhile, Dracula, though a prisoner, was mainly treated as an honored guest. After being left to cool off for a bit in Buda Castle's dungeon, he spent much of the next 12 years (1462-1474) under house arrest at Matthias' palace at Visegrád on the Danube. With Dracula's wings clipped and his inability to have insolent people skewered with the nod of his head, historians and portraitists began arriving to get a load of the great Impaler first-hand. These visits are the source of most of the physical descriptions and paintings of Vlad that we have today.

With the political ramifications of executing Vlad being too detrimental to even consider, the ever-resourceful Matthias began using Dracula as a kind of living, breathing, tooth-gnashing deterrent. When Turkish delegations visited the Hungarian court[130], Dracula was prominently stationed in the room during negotiations. The sight of the glowering, nostril-flaring Impaler presumably caused more than a few spontaneous bladder evacuations among the diplomats. The message, of course, was that Matthias had the dreaded Dracula locked and loaded for another round of Ottoman impaling if Mehmed ever decided to screw with him.

---

[130] Which seems just a little too blatantly incriminating, considering Matthias' delicate circumstances.

Dracula can't have been too thrilled about being paraded around as Matthias' junkyard dog, but with support for his case dwindling and what was left of his guard hopelessly out of touch, he must have had to draw upon heroic willpower to not set upon Matthias with a butter knife at these affairs and furnish him with a few new orifices.

Meanwhile, though Matthias' ambitions to worm his way into the shoes of emperor had failed, after years of merely being designated as provisional King of Hungary, he finally completed his legitimate crowning by literally buying the holy crown of St. Stephan of Hungary from Frederick III.

While Matthias was now king without question or challenge, this event once again invited the unhappy eyes of Rome and Venice to be cast down upon him. That crusading money he'd been given had pretty obviously been used to facilitate his acquisition of the crown. Pope Pius had died and been replaced by the financially diligent Pope Paul II, and he was downright perturbed about the misuse of his office's funds, letting Matthias know that he owed his position to the papacy. As the pope tightened the screws on Matthias to finally make good on his crusading promises, incentive for him to act was simultaneously emerging from the east.

Stephen of Moldavia had shaken off his defeat from two years earlier and was still of a mind to do more damage to those bastard Hungarians, plus simultaneously dispense with stupid Radu and install his own protégé in Wallachia. To that end, he once again attacked the key Wallachian fortress at Chilia in 1465. Matthias, who apparently really liked having that fortress at his disposal through his partnership with Radu, retaliated first and lost badly in 1467, getting seriously wounded in the process. Then Radu stepped up to save face over Stephen taking his fortress. The culminating battle, however, didn't occur until 1473 near Bucharest. Even with Turkish backup, Radu lost his nerve, abandoned his forces, and hid in Bucharest fortress. With the Wallachians and Turks now leaderless, it was easy work for Stephen's crew to wipe out the remaining forces and take the city. As was custom, to the victors went the spoils. Stephen happily scooped up all of Radu's treasures, vestments, and flags, even capturing Radu's wife and daughter[131]. He replaced Radu with Basarab Laiotă, yet another contender for the throne from the seemingly inexhaustible Dăneşti clan, who then made his own deal with the Turks.

Radu eventually collected himself and continued throwing troops at Stephen and Basarb, but to no avail. Radu's woeful resistance eventually lost the support of ever-fickle Hungary and he soon died of syphilis in 1475.

Matthias had lost his man in Wallachia and therefore any sort of agreement with the Ottomans. Once again he faced the real possibility of the Turks taking a shot at Buda. It was time to declare a Code D(racula).

---

[131] Stephan later married the girl, as one does.

In July 1475, Matthias made Dracula an offer he couldn't refuse: fight the Turks for Hungary and regain his throne in Wallachia or die as prisoner. After 12 years of twiddling his thumbs at the palace at Visegrád, with short intervals of playing Ottoman boogeyman in Buda, the PSI needle on Vlad's rage gauge must have been buried in the red. Unable to bury a dagger handle-deep into Matthias' eye socket, he took the offer as the next best thing.

Matthias locked down the terms of their relationship by making Vlad convert to Roman Catholicism and marry his cousin. The marriage was evidently consummated 10 seconds later, because the first of two sons was born while Dracula was still in Buda getting his ducks in a row for an eventual crusade.

Meanwhile, news spread that Dracula was back in the game and absolved by Matthias of the German accusations from years earlier. Still considered a living legend, there was much fist-pumping going on in Europe, particularly Venice and Rome. Their boy Dracula was about get back to what he did best: literally scaring the shit out of the Turks.

The pace was stepped up considerably as Mehmed's ambitions had once again inspired him to dip uncomfortably close to Hungarian and Transylvanian territory, including Bosnia and Crimea. Matthias, maddeningly cautious as always, went through the motions of making sure it was cool with all the Hungarian nobles that he go full bore into the conflict with the Turks, raised funds, gathered weapons and materials, and finally in January 1476 it was clobbering time for Dracula.

While newly elected Pope Sixtus rallied forces in Italy, as well as Central and Eastern Europe, Stephen of Moldavia, belatedly feeling remorse for having betrayed his cousin Vlad and having quickly lost faith in Basarab, actively campaigned to have Dracula reinstalled in Wallachia. He even sent an envoy to Buda, where his name couldn't have been too popular, to advocate for Dracula directly to Matthias.

Matthias wasn't *quite* ready to hand Dracula the keys to Wallachia, so instead he formally released Dracula[132], appointed him captain, and the two headed for Bosnia to do some Ottoman exterminating. After liberating just one city, Matthias, gripped in his customary post-victory swoon, returned to Buda to do a little partying and left Dracula in charge. Without a chaperone, Dracula started making up for lost time by shaking off the rust on his killing, mutilating, burning and looting skills.

Though Dracula's victims undoubtedly besieged Matthias' complaints department, it was difficult to argue with his record, which by now included liberating (and then looting) several more Bosnian cities. Matthias and Hungary gave Vlad the nod to gallop into Wallachia and take back his throne—with supervision, of course.

---

[132] Fun fact: Dracula ultimately spent almost twice as many years in "jail" as he did as prince of Wallachia.

Dracula and some 21,000 men were led by the militarily incompetent, but demonstrably not crazy, Stephen Báthory[133]. After an unplanned detour to aid Stephen of Moldavia's army, which had been ambushed by a Turkish contingent (Dracula's forces swooped in and decisively pounded them), the united forces headed for a showdown with Basarab in Wallachia. They stopped briefly in Braşov where, with the help of an amazingly persuasive diplomat from Matthias' court, Dracula was able to mend fences with local authorities. To sweeten the deal, Dracula gave them previously unknown freedom to do unrestricted business in Wallachia and made several lucrative trade agreements between the two regions.

While Stephen attacked Wallachia from the east, Dracula attacked from the north, running headlong into Basarab's army of 18,000 men, mainly made up of Turks. Dracula's army won, though both sides suffered incredible losses.

Dracula pressed on, now heading for Bucharest while Stephen's forces flattened any Turkish resistance from the opposite direction. They converged on Bucharest and by November 26, 1476, Dracula was again Prince of Wallachia.

After celebrating a job well done, Báthory and Stephen withdrew with their forces, which seems like a

---

[133] Great uncle to Elizabeth Báthory, "The Blood Countess" (1560-1614), who is said to have killed some 650 girls whose blood she used for cosmetics and bathing, which she thought kept her skin looking emollient. Her legend provided yet more inspiration and material for Dracula and vampire writers.

premature move even to a military dummy like me. Báthory was celebrated in Buda and eventually given governorship of Transylvania, and Pope Sixtus bestowed on Stephen the title "Stephen the Great and Holy"[134].

Poor Dracula was once again left alone with a dangerously insufficient army on the front lines against the seemingly boundless Ottoman hoarde. Unsurprisingly, barely two months later, near the end of December 1476, Dracula was dead.

---

[134] Aka "the Champion of Christ," a.k.a. "Athleta Christi."

# Snagov, Dracula's Dirt Nap

According to legend, Dracula's body was found in a marsh near Snagov Monastery, located about 40 kilometers (25 miles) north of Bucharest, on an island in Lake Snagov. His head was gone, bouncing in a bag on the back of a horse sprinting toward a giddy Mehmed in Constantinople, and the rest of his body had clearly been wailed on before being dumped.

Stephen the Great, perhaps out of guilt for his previous betrayals against his cousin, had left an elite force of 200 bodyguards to help fortify Dracula's pitiable remaining ranks, which were said to number barely 4,000. All but 10 of these bodyguards died in battle, and the survivors were later able to limp back to the Moldavian court in Suceava and relay the final moments of Dracula's life.

The divergent stories of Vlad's last days include:

Basarab had somehow avoided the usual extravagant death that Vlad saved for enemies of his stature and was able to round up an astounding number of Ottoman soldiers to retaliate. Bucharest fortress, for all its incredible sturdiness, was just too close to the Danube for comfort. Vlad and his forces retreated to the marshes near Snagov for a bit more wiggle room, but it made no difference. Basarab's forces smashed them in short order.

In another account of his death, this one recorded by an Austrian chronicler, the Turks used Vlad's own trick against him, sending an assassin dressed as a servant into Vlad's camp. This person was able to kill him, remove his head and somehow escape unnoticed, while presumably covered in all the blood, bone, and goo that accompanies a quick and dirty decapitating.

Other theories about Dracula's death include that he was killed by the perpetually duplicitous Wallachian boyars[135]; killed in battle with the Turks; or he was accidentally killed by one of his own men who mistook him for a Turk, just as he was about to taste victory in yet another skirmish. Common sense suggests the latter story seems iffy. If Dracula died surrounded by his own men, it's difficult to believe they would have allowed the Turks to get hold of the body, decapitate and mutilate it.

One way or another, we know Vlad's head was delivered to a visibly relieved Sultan Mehmed by January 10, 1477, preserved in honey, then staked and displayed somewhere prominent.

------------------------------------

Snagov Monastery (*Manastirea Snagov*) is long believed to be the final resting place of (the rest of) Vlad Dracula. The church dates from 1364 and, like his father before him, Vlad lavished money on the place, first for atonement and later for defense. As a good Orthodox man—but not really, who are we kidding?—it's assumed that Dracula subscribed to the

---

[135] Unlikely, since anyone who still opposed Dracula when he reclaimed his throne, knowing his usual methods of dealing with disloyal people, probably had the good sense to hightail it for the mountains.

popular idea at the time that one could literally repay the spiritual debt from one's evil-doings by pouring money into building and improving monasteries, which Vlad did all over Wallachia.

However, Dracula wasn't a friend to all churches. The encroachment of various Roman Catholic monasteries in his realm irritated Vlad to no end, being that they were established by the Hungarian king and were thus effectively little religious communes immune to Dracula's rule. Vlad had disputes with many of the Catholic abbots and monks—by which I mean he destroyed their monasteries and staked them as petty acts of ego maintenance that probably didn't help his reputation back in Buda.

But Snagov was extremely important to Vlad (and his father) and he visited frequently. Dracula would roll up, likely having come straight from some horrific venture, smoke a doobie, chill out, seek spiritual guidance, presumably confess all his stake-wielding sins and, on at least one occasion, hide from raging Turks.

As Vlad became more preoccupied with defense, he financed the fortification of the monastery. Vlad saw Snagov as an outstanding natural refuge, being in the middle of a dense forest and surrounded on all sides by water, which allowed for excellent views in every direction. In 1458 Vlad oversaw the construction of massive walls around the perimeter of the entire island, greatly enlarging the monastery's area and transforming it into a combination town-fortress, with princely residences, houses for wealthy boyars, stables, a prison, vaults for treasure, a printing press, a dungeon/torture chamber, and other decidedly non-pious accoutrements that had no business being in a monastery. One assumes the on-duty abbot's head nigh on smoked with cognitive dissonance.

One of Dracula's pimped-out additions to the property allegedly included a trapdoor in front of a Virgin Mary icon. Vlad would lead whatever miscreant was bothering him that week to this icon, and when the unknowing victim knelt to worship, Dracula would activate the trapdoor, dropping the victim into a deep hole with stakes jammed vertically into the floor. Death was more or less instantaneous (if he was lucky) from a gravity-assisted multi-impalement. It's said decapitated skeletons have been found at Snagov, supporting the trapdoor tale.

It's also rumored that Dracula constructed a secret tunnel under the lake to connect the monastery with the mainland—presumably as a panic escape route. With the unbridled polygamy of the time, however, I'm sure he found other uses for it.

Among the many Dracula-related legends around Snagov that still persist is the one about a hidden treasure in the area, apparently still waiting to be discovered. As the tale goes, when the Ottoman threat mushroomed and his untimely, messy death seemed imminent, Vlad allegedly had soldiers and villagers build cast-iron barrels in which he sealed silver, gold and jewels. He then had a river dammed and diverted long enough to bury these barrels in the riverbed. After he removed the dam, the site was flooded with water again. Finally, allegedly, Vlad impaled everyone involved in executing this plan for good measure[136], so there was no chance anyone would blab. Never mind how he impaled all these people singlehandedly without someone running off and coming back with a cannon to shoot Vlad in the face.

-------------------------------

Snagov looks nothing like its fortified incarnation today. Without the constant threat of being hog-piled by Turks, Russians or whomever, the island eventually demilitarized down to something more closely approximating, you know, a monastery. The fortifications are now gone as well as most of the historic homes, prison and such. Apart from residences and outbuildings, what remains is just the church and ancient remnants of monks' quarters. Neagoe Basarab[137] built the current iteration of the church between 1517 and 1521 in the Byzantine style that had become trendy. The exterior is done in decorative bricks, with four short towers. Many of the interior murals covering the walls, columns, and ceiling were painted in 1563, with a few surviving 15th-century images of the ruling family. These murals, dominated by an incredible assortment of saints[138], have undergone several restorations over the centuries.

---

[136] Because simply, humanely wanging them on the head with a frying pan wouldn't suffice.
[137] Prince of Wallachia from 1512 to 1521.
[138] And, boy, are there a lot of saints!

----------------------------------

The legend that Dracula was buried here gained momentum sometime in the 19th century, the main evidence being a stone slab on the floor, presumably marking a tomb, dead-center at the front of the church and just in front of the altar. Whatever inscriptions the stone slab originally displayed have long since worn away under the shuffling feet of monks[139], but a plaque had materialized claiming to mark the Prince's grave.

Considering Vlad's long relationship with Snagov, the story certainly had merit. For some time, one of the many stories/theories regarding the circumstances of Vlad's death was that he was killed by janissaries[140] in nearby woods during a battle, then buried by his subjects somewhere on the grounds of Snagov.

Burial stones had previously been dug up around the property, but a mix of horse, ox, and human bones were all that was found. In 1933 researchers were allowed to dig up the slab by the altar only to find an empty chamber (no casket), more animal bones, ceramics and even a few archeological finds dating back to the Iron Age.

Another tomb slab near the church door, a highly unusual place for a tomb, was dug up. This encouragingly

---

[139] Or, it's argued, possibly sanded off by an abbot years later, who presumably wanted to downplay Snagov's association with Vlad Țepeș Dracula.

[140] Mentioned previously, these were Turkish infantry who had been kidnapped from their homelands, trained, and forced into Ottoman military service.

*did* have a casket inside, one covered by a tattered purple pall with gold embroidery. The casket contained a headless body, dressed quite regally in silk, a crimson shirt and silver buttons. Also, in the grave were fragments of a crown, a woman's ring (minus the gem), a cup, and a buckle made partly of gold.

After some excited theorizing, it was believed this was indeed Dracula's remains and that at some stage, possibly while Greeks, who were known to have had no love for the Prince, were overseeing the monastery, an abbot had exhumed and moved the body from the altar-side tomb to near the door. This move could have been precipitated by the belief that Vlad was simply too evil to be that close to the altar, and therefore God. More importantly, he had converted to Catholicism, which probably didn't go over too well with the Orthodox monks. Or perhaps the move was motivated by pure spite, as this grave by the entrance would be constantly trod upon by visitors as a kind of post-mortem, ceaseless dishonoring.

More sober consideration later cast doubt on the theory that these remains belonged to Dracula. For starters, there was no mural or portrait of Vlad anywhere in the church, which is commonly installed when someone is interred. Such an impermanent marking could have easily been painted over or scrubbed away by the same no-goodniks believed to have moved Vlad's remains, but that's only a guess. Later, the still unidentified remains found in the tomb by the door quietly disappeared from the History Museum of Bucharest. Thus, the legend continued.

A new theory was floated by a monk in 1975 during an interview with the Associated Press. The monk had a hunch that the tomb by the altar did indeed contain Dracula's remains; they were just buried extra, super-duper deep to defeat grave robbers. There were also undoubtedly former rivals to dupe, enemies who might want a second crack at the corpse believing that simple death and decapitation wasn't nearly punishment enough for their old nemesis.

An American team of archeologists asked the Romanian government for permission to do more digging on this spot, but they were denied, allegedly due to safety concerns after earthquakes in 1940 and 1977 had destabilized the church's foundation.

More discouraging was that if Dracula had been buried at Snagov, any evidence had probably been long since stolen or destroyed by any number of people over the centuries, including Vlad-hating abbots and monks, looters and/or vandals, particularly during a period in the early 19th century when the monastery was all but abandoned.

For some time in the late-90s and early-2000s, no one was able to research the burial site further, because the world's angriest abbot wouldn't let anyone near the supposed grave. Travelers' and journalists' encounters with this guy became a kind of legend of its own. Anyone who showed up hoping to tiptoe in and at least gaze on the slab was invariably intercepted, told to jump up their own asses and leave (or language roughly that harsh, according to anecdotes).

At some stage, a light went on in someone's head and the church's caretakers started allowing visitors to tour the church again, charging a fee to take photographs, naturally.

The final resting place of Vlad Ţepeş Dracula is still unknown. It's now widely believed that the Turks buried him unceremoniously at Comana, a monastery founded by Vlad in 1461. Alas, Comana was destroyed and rebuilt in 1589. If Vlad ever had a grave marker, it's long gone.

In 2014, speculation about Vlad's final resting place was rekindled after the discovery of a tomb with Dracula-ish symbols—a dragon and two opposing sphinxes—in the same Naples cemetery where Vlad's daughter and son-in-law are buried. This fueled theories that Dracula hadn't died in battle, but had instead been captured alive by the Turks, ransomed to his daughter who was married to a Neapolitan count, and eventually died in Italy. This theory, though well circulated around the click-bait corners of the internet, has so many holes that it hasn't thus far gained any legitimate traction.

As of this writing, there were still no plausible theories as to the true fate of Vlad's body and no known individual(s) actively working on the mystery.

# Down for the Count

"We are in Transylvania, and Transylvania is not England.
Our ways are not your ways, and there shall be to you many
strange things."
- *Dracula*

Almost 500 years after his death, the name "Dracula" was
plucked out of near obscurity by an Irish novelist who had
never set foot in Romania and, some argue, was only
marginally aware of his antagonist's namesake.

Before we get to how profoundly a fictional literary
character has affected Romania's identity and tourism
strategy, if you've never read the novel or, like me, you tend
to forget three-quarters of most books as soon as you put
them down, I'll indulge you with a refresher summary of the
story. Though I promise it'll be entertaining, those of you
who would rather skip this summery can zap down and start
reading after the line of '§'s.

------------------------------------

If you haven't read *Dracula*, it's important to know there is
no in-scene narrative or action in the entire novel. Instead,
all events are narrated via a series of letters, journal entries,
and a few ships' logs. These are supplemented by newspaper
clippings to reveal events not directly witnessed by any of

the characters. This literary style was undoubtedly an edgy choice in Bram Stoker's time, and particularly effective for a reading audience that was not already as familiar with popular vampire themes as we are today. For 21st-century readers, however, it can sometimes make for glacial plot progression.

We open with the introduction of our first protagonist, sweet, perilously naïve Jonathan Harker, a recently lawyered lad from the mild streets of 1893 England. We learn via his correspondence to his fiancée Wilhelmina Murray, wisely nicknamed "Mina," that Jonathan is on a slow train/carriage voyage to the so-called Castle Dracula in Transylvania near the border with Moldavia, to meet and close a real estate deal that his boss facilitated with the nobleman Count Dracula[141].

As Harker gets closer to the castle, learning of his destination, the local peasants express unanimous alarm, warning him to turn back and, when he doesn't, loading him down with crucifixes and other anti-evil doohickeys. This is also when Harker first hears an unusual word, which he later translates into "vampire."

The chorus of beseeching eventually activates the previously inert part of Harker's brain that processes the get-the-fuck-out instinct, but apparently the lawyer job

---

[141] Pompous ass named the castle after himself. Is *that* where Trump got the idea?

market in the 1890s was pretty tight, because he dutifully presses on to fulfill his obligation to his boss.

The Count sends a carriage to ferry Harker through the last leg of his journey through the Borgo Pass. This is presumably to keep him from scream-running all the way back to England when he gets a load of the Dark Forest of Urethra Failure[142], where the carriage seems to be going in circles and is persistently stalked by howling, gnashing wolves. Knees knocking at 137 beats per minute, Harker finally arrives at the large, crumbling Castle Dracula.

To Harker's mild and very temporary relief, despite being noticeably pale, gaunt, sporting pointy ears and very prominent canine teeth, Count Dracula proves to be a charming and hospitable host. He also appears to be living in the castle alone, which Harker surmises after witnessing Dracula singlehandedly cooking, serving, and cleaning up the meals, and even attending to the bedding in his guestroom. Harker's composure starts to dissolve when, after cutting himself while shaving—funny story, the castle has no mirrors—Dracula barely controls the urge to pounce on his bloody throat.

Despite satisfying almost every bullet-point on the serial-killer checklist, it takes a few days of creepy confinement and increasingly harsh guest rules for Harker to figure out that he's more prisoner than visitor. Full-fledged panic ensues as Harker realizes that Dracula

---

[142] Not its real name.

possesses a variety of supernatural powers and feeds on the blood of the living. Also, surprise! He seems to have a diabolical master plan regarding his real estate purchase and imminent trip to England that involves sampling the local, ahem, *culinary options* and, presumably, a bold power-grab in a society with more luster than some scattered Transylvanian villages.

While inspecting one of the Count's many off-limits rooms one evening for a possible escape route, Harker stumbles upon and is then attacked by three gorgeous, horny, and presumably hungry female vampires. Now, if one hypothetically *had* to be murdered and blood-drained, I can think of worse ways to go, but before any of that Penthouse Forum action takes place, Dracula swoops in and informs the undead harem that Harker "belongs" to him. Harker realizes he's being kept alive only to complete their business deal (and idle snacking) and then Dracula plans to drain him down to a lawyer-shaped raisin.

Experiencing crescendoing terror about his confinement, and definitely being opposed to Dracula's implied guy-on-guy, homoerotic, blood-bath execution, Harker attempts and fails to kill the Count. Dracula, opting to bypass this stubborn quick snack in favor of an all-he-can-eat buffet, departs for England, hauling 50 boxes of Transylvanian earth with him. Harker, low on blood, weak, and delirious, manages to escape the castle by shimmying down the exterior walls.

Cut to England. As Dracula has been intercepting all of Jonathan Harker's increasingly fearful letters, a concerned Mina Murray is unaware that her fiancé has been held hostage, never mind that he came within a whisker of being the main course in a kind of vampire Thanksgiving S&M orgy.

We learn via correspondence[143] that Mina Murray's good friend, Lucy Westenra, has received three marriage proposals in quick succession from Dr. John Seward, who runs an insane asylum in London; Arthur Holmwood, a friend and future Lord; and Quincey Morris, who apparently becomes instantly enamored with Lucy while visiting Arthur from Texas. He soon, somewhat dickishly, attempts a nuptial end-run around his friend.

Lucy, either amazingly sincere or humble-bragging the living ca-ca out of the situation, expresses remorse that she can't reverse-Mormon the situation and accept all three men before deciding to accept her friend Arthur Holmwood's offer. Mina temporarily forgets her fiancé has gone missing in the European equivalent of the Appalachian Mountains, becomes embroiled in Lucy's faux dilemma, and travels to join her friend at the seaside town of Whitby to ostensibly console her through this embarrassment of whipped-guy options.

While Mina is visiting Lucy in Whitby, a Russian ship runs ashore near the town. It's revealed that the ship,

---

[143] These people do nothing but write letters and journal all day long.

originating from the Black Sea port of Varna, has no crew and its captain is found dead, lashed to the ship's wheel, armed with a crucifix, and looking none too happy about his final moments.

While officials investigate this bizarre situation, a "large dog"[144] hurdles out of its hiding place on the ship, leaps to shore and dashes into the countryside. The captain's increasingly urgent logs tell the tale of the crew spotting a tall, thin stowaway, a man they cannot find during a thorough search. Then, one-by-one, the crew start to go missing during their voyage and the captain, fully expecting to be disappeared himself, ties himself to the wheel in a last ditch-effort to steer the ship to land before this fate befalls him. The ship's only cargo is fifty boxes of earth shipped from Castle Dracula. Apparently having no reason to believe the cargo and the doomed ship's fate are somehow related, the boxes are duly delivered to a newly purchased home in London.

Soon after, Lucy resumes her old habit of chronic sleepwalking. Except now she's *distance* sleepwalking. One night, learning that Lucy has wandered off, Mina finds her friend hanging out in her nightgown on a bench near the town cemetery. As she approaches, Mina catches a glimpse of a tall, dark form with glowing red eyes bent over Lucy, but the black shape vanishes by the time Mina reaches her. Mina

---

[144] Guess who?

notices two bloody pricks on her friend's neck. Lucy remembers nothing.

In the ensuing nights, Lucy keeps wandering off. Once she's found lingering at her open window, another time in bed with what appears to be a giant bat flapping in the room. Lucy's health begins to deteriorate over the next few weeks.

Arthur summons Dr. Seward, who's been at his asylum in London tending to an increasingly difficult patient called Renfield who's been eating bugs and birds believing that he'll absorb their life-force and obsessing over an invisible "master." Seward races up to Whitby, probably because he's a tireless gentleman, but perhaps hoping some timely life-saving heroics will inspire Lucy to change her mind about his proposal—or that Arthur might trip in front of a streetcar while preoccupied by distress. Seward can't explain Lucy's bizarre condition and decides to call in someone who knows a thing or two about freaky afflictions, his old friend and mentor Professor Van Helsing.

As if she weren't already creeped out enough, Mina learns that a sick and half-mad Jonathan Harker has somehow staggered all the way to Budapest, having been hospitalized with a kind of "brain fever." Mina leaves immediately to attend to him.

Van Helsing travels from his home in Amsterdam to Whitby with startling speed for 1893, examines Lucy, and recognizes her vampire-esque symptoms. The men start administering blood transfusions to Lucy in an effort to counteract her mysterious loss of blood, despite no overt wounds apart from the two tiny pricks on her neck. To everyone's relief, Lucy begins to recover. Van Helsing drapes Lucy's entire bedroom with garlic, including a wreath around her neck, suggesting that it will help her condition without explaining his diagnosis to the others.

Unfortunately, Lucy's busybody, clean-freak mother, who didn't get the memo about the garlic, decides to tidy up. In the grand tradition of moms everywhere throwing out treasured record collections and valuable comic books, she removes the smelly garlic adornments from Lucy's room without a moment's thought as to what the hell they were doing there in the first place. Then she opens the window to air out the room. When Van Helsing and Seward return in the morning, Lucy is once again near death. More blood transfusions ensue and Lucy shows improvement.

A few nights later, a wolf that has escaped the local Zoological Gardens breaks into the house by smashing through Lucy's bedroom window. Lucy's mother is literally scared to death due to an existing heart condition, leaving Lucy completely defenseless to more attacks.

Lucy is found once again near death and, curiously, sporting prominent canine teeth that Van Helsing hadn't noticed earlier. He summons Arthur Holmwood, who has been off attending to his father's death, to say goodbye to his fading fiancée. Lucy makes a brief, uncharacteristically seductive plea for Arthur to kiss her, but Van Helsing warns that he should only kiss her forehead. Arthur does this, Lucy dies and, peculiarly, regains her pre-illness appearance.

After Lucy's burial, the local newspapers begin reporting that local children are being stalked and attacked by "a beautiful woman." Seward summons Arthur Holmwood and the still-lingering Quincey Morris, then Van Helsing finally explains to the group that Lucy is most likely a mindless and extremely hungry vampire. After an understandable amount of debate and convincing evidence, everyone is on the same page and they resolve to kill the Lucy-pire—for real this time.

The men track down and find Lucy, who's just finished dining on a child. Poor Arthur Holmwood—already well past any hope of sanity-saving therapy—gets the unenviable task of staking his ex-fiancée through the heart. They all work together to cut off Lucy's head and stuff her mouth with garlic. After the men presumably take a moment to barf up their last three meals, they resolve to destroy Dracula himself.

Having gotten married in Budapest, as one does soon after a near-death experience with sexy vampires, Jonathan and Mina return to England and learn of Lucy's death. Van Helsing, Seward, Arthur, and Quincey travel to London to join Harker and Mina. Harker shares the bad news about Count Dracula's powers and plans, and they form a kind of "Avengers" team to deal with the vampire.

Van Helsing briefs everyone on the legend of the nosferatu and his powers, including immortality, incredible strength, the ability to command various animals and the elements, and vanish/change form at will. The Un-Dead's weaknesses include: they can't survive without blood, can't enter a house/building without the invitation of a mortal, and they lose their powers during the day, thus for their safety they must seek shelter in the earth or a coffin filled with earth. They are also powerless against crucifixes, Communion wafers, and other holy objects.

Since the group has been journaling their little hearts out the entire time, including Harker who amazingly had the wherewithal to bring his Transylvania diary with him during his escape, Mina and Van Helsing collect everyone's journals to piece together a single knowledge-base in preparation for their showdown with the Count.

Fully briefed on Dracula, his apparent powers and weaknesses, and his grand design to make England his new banquet table, the team starts tracking down the aforementioned boxes of Transylvanian earth stashed around London, which the Count needs for naptime as foreign (read: English) earth won't rejuvenate him. They quickly find several boxes and contaminate the earth inside. Meanwhile, Dracula has become aware that Van Helsing and his team are not only on his trail, but actually have a viable plan to kill him.

While the group is staying at Dr. Seward's asylum in London, poor, troubled Renfield, still entranced by Dracula, invites the vampire into the building. Dracula sucks on Mina, for what is apparently the second or third time, and then feeds her his own blood, giving her the vampire infection.

With Mina now transforming into a vampire, time becomes a factor. Van Helsing is certain they can save Mina by destroying Dracula. The team splits up and continues to track down and sully Dracula's boxes of Transylvanian earth, leaving him nowhere to safely sleep. While Harker and Van Helsing are contaminating one cache of boxes, Dracula confronts them. It's daytime, meaning Dracula is powerless. But unlike contemporary vampire characters, Dracula can in fact survive outside during the day if he's suitably covered up. He quickly surmises that he's outmatched and escapes. Dracula flees England, resolving to live and feed on young, English babes another day, heading home to Transylvania with his last box of uncontaminated earth.

Mina, who is now mentally connected to Dracula through some kind of vampire Wi-Fi, begins to have visions. Her companions quickly realize these are actually a conduit to the Count himself. They are able to deduce that Dracula is traveling back to Transylvania by sea.

The team boards the Orient Express in the hopes of beating Dracula's boat to Varna and ambushing him. However, it turns out that vampire Wi-Fi, unsurprisingly, works both ways; Dracula becomes aware of his pursuers and has the boat change course to dock at Galatz, farther north. The Avengers just miss Dracula disembarking at Galatz and they decide to split up and continue pursuit— Mina and Van Helsing by train, Arthur and Harker upriver by steamboat, and Seward and Quincey through the countryside on horseback.

Van Helsing and Mina arrive at Castle Dracula first, where they encounter the three female vampires. Van Helsing heroically resists their compelling invitations for toothy sexual adventure and kills them all. He then uses vampire-repellent objects to seal all the castle entrances, effectively leaving the Count locked out of his own refuge.

But before the Count has the chance to cope with that little surprise, Harker, Quincey, Arthur, and Seward catch up with the group of gypsies transporting the box containing Dracula to his castle. With the sun setting, they have no time to dillydally. The men overpower the gypsies, Quincey is wounded in the scuffle, and they wrench the box open. Dracula is awake and senses he's moments away from having the power to feed these insolent humans their own private parts. In a flash, Harker beheads Dracula while Quincey stabs him in the heart. Dracula undergoes a spectacularly rapid swing of emotion from "near triumph" to "oh fuck," before crumbling into a pile of ash. Quincey succumbs to his injury and dies. Mina returns to normal, as Van Helsing predicted.

Flash to seven years later. Harker and Mina are amazingly living PTSD-free and happily ever after, with their child who goes by the name "Quincey." Seward and Arthur are also happily married.

The end.

§§§§§§§§§§§§§§§§§§§§§§§§§§§§§§§§§§§§§§§§§§§§§§§§§

Abraham Stoker was born in Dublin on November 8, 1847[145].
In addition to being an admirably prolific writer, he spent
the bulk of his career working as the business manager for
the Lyceum Theatre in London, a double-duty job that
included serving as personal assistant to the theatre's owner,
the idiosyncratic, renowned actor Henry Irving.

Stoker's first published piece of fiction was "The
Crystal Cup," which was published in the *London Society* in
1872. Other pieces of fiction and non-fiction followed,
including the blistering page-turner "The Duties of Clerks of
Petty Sessions in Ireland" (1879), written during his nearly
10-year stint as a civil servant. Stoker eventually started
moonlighting as a lowly theatre critic, which, after dashing
off a glowing review about one of Irving's productions, is
how he eventually came to know and later be employed by
the actor.

Stoker married Florence Balcombe in 1878, after
winning her away from the unlikely wooing of one Oscar
Wilde[146]. The Stokers soon moved to London so Bram could
start his career as business manager at the Lyceum, where
he stayed for 27 years. The struggling Lyceum would develop

---

[145] Let's all take a moment to breathe a sigh of relief that he didn't choose
the decidedly non-Gothic "Abe" as his nickname.
[146] Wilde eventually mended ties with Stoker and the two remained
friends, even after Wilde's disastrous fall from grace in the U.K. and exile
in France.

into a hugely successful theatre while under the supervision of Irving and Stoker.

Working with Irving was Stoker's door into London's high society and a bit of world travel as well. Work took the two to the U.S., where Stoker was twice invited to the White House as Irving's +1, and he also had the opportunity to meet one of his literary idols, Walt Whitman. Stoker later used his experiences in America for material in two novels set in the U.S. These feature Americans as characters, including a fellow by the name of Quincey Morris, who was recycled in *Dracula*.

It wasn't until 1890 that Stoker visited the English town of Whitby, when it's believed he was first inspired to write *Dracula*. Stoker had already gotten his feet wet in long-form writing during the Lyceum years with *The Snake's Pass*, published that same year.

Speaking as an oft over-extended writer, I can say with all authority that Stoker somehow finding the time to work on several books between his relentless duties at the theatre is a heroic feat comparable to single-handedly designing and building a four-seat aircraft while serving as the President of the United States.

Stoker spent roughly seven years researching, cultivating, and writing *Dracula*. His work included studying European folklore and mythological stories of vampires, as well as at least two meetings with Professor Ármin Vámbéry from Budapest who, some theorize, shared some of the darker tales of Transylvania's Carpathian Mountains with Stoker. *Dracula* was published in 1897.

The novel's style, narrated entirely via the protagonists' diary entries, letters, telegrams, ship's logs, and newspaper clippings—writing styles Stoker honed as a newspaper writer—served to enhance the story's sense of realism for the reading audience of the time. Today, that kind of slow plot progression and scarcity of antagonist action would appeal only to the most forgiving of readers. Admittedly, I've seen way too many car chases and Marvel superhero movies, so it's possible my brain has become the consistency of stale oatmeal, requiring constant stimulation to keep it from wandering and skimming for the next explosion.

Fun fact: The original 541-page typed manuscript for *Dracula*, including the original title, *"The Un-Dead,"* handwritten on the title page and featuring an alternate ending, was somehow misplaced and was believed to be lost forever. It wasn't found until the early 1980s, in a barn in northwestern Pennsylvania of all places[147]. This manuscript was bought at auction by an unnamed person, later revealed to be Paul Allen, co-founder of Microsoft, who has thus far opted to keep it under his pillow, or wherever billionaires hide their fetish possessions instead of making them available for public display.

---

[147] I can't be the first person who has noted the eeriness of a lost manuscript of a novel set in Transylvania being found in Pennsylvania, right? I mean, how many 'nsylvania's are there?

After completing *Dracula*, Stoker continued his remarkable writing output, serving as part of the literary staff of *The Daily Telegraph* and publishing other works of fiction, including the horror novels *The Lady of the Shroud* (1909) and *The Lair of the White Worm* (1911). Stoker also wrote the somber tribute *Personal Reminiscences of Henry Irving* after his boss' death in 1905.

Stoker died on April 20, 1912. His health had severely degraded after suffering a series of strokes, which may have been accompanied by tertiary syphilis, though this was never confirmed. Another compelling theory for Stoker's deterioration was overwork, which seems plausible, considering his writing productivity and tireless work for the Lyceum. He was cremated and his ashes placed in a display urn at Golders Green Crematorium in London. Visitors can still view the urn today.

Like so many artists before and after him, Stoker tragically enjoyed only modest literary success while he was alive. Indeed, he was so poor near the end of his life that he had to appeal for a compassionate grant from the Royal Literary Fund to survive[148]. A few years after his death, his wife Florence, flirting with destitution herself, sold Stoker's *Dracula* notes and outlines for a pitiful 2 pounds. Today these are housed in the Rosenbach Museum and Library in Philadelphia, Pennsylvania[149].

---

[148] The contemporary version of this desperation tactic is called "getting a part-time job at a coffee shop."

[149] Oddly, not the same copy found in the Pennsylvania barn.

Stoker is, of course, now considered one of Ireland's greatest authors. Dublin holds an annual Bram Stoker Festival each fall honoring his literary achievements, funded by the Bram Stoker Estate, Dublin City Council and the Irish national tourism body Failte Ireland.

---------------------------------------------

Considering that Count Dracula only appears on 62 of the 390 pages of the novel, barely speaks and, when he does, shares sparing details about his motivations and almost nothing about his origin, the character's enduring popularity is kind of astonishing. However, as I hinted earlier, the novel wasn't a hit right out of the gate, despite widespread critical praise. Sir Arthur Conan Doyle, author of *Sherlock Holmes*, even sent a personal congratulatory letter to Stoker, saying "I write to tell you how very much I have enjoyed reading *Dracula*. I think it is the very best story of diablerie which I have read for many years."

It wasn't until after people started producing vampire films in the 1920s, many years after Stoker's death, that *Dracula* exploded onto the general reading audiences' radar. It was F. W. Murnau's unauthorized adaptation of the novel in the film "Nosferatu," which debuted in 1922, that helped bring fame to *Dracula*. The studio didn't or couldn't (it's unclear) get rights to the story from Florence, who was now acting as Bram's literary executor, so they changed just enough names and details in the film to put themselves in the litigious clear. Or so they thought. Florence Stoker went after them anyway, and it was the press coverage of the ensuing legal circus that caused the novel's popularity to finally spike. Florence was ultimately successful in her lawsuit against Murnau, which resulted in all prints and negatives of "Nosferatu" being destroyed, though as we know, some prints survived and the film eventually achieved classic status of its own.

The novel's second life in the literary world opened the door for a wildly successful stage adaptation, which toured the U.K. for three years before hopping over for a U.S. tour. Hollywood pounced and an American film based on the book was released in 1931, starring Bela Lugosi, coincidentally a native of Romania, whom I'll discuss later.

*Dracula* was already popular in the U.S. due to yet more legal snafus. Stoker, with flakiness typical of a freelance writer, failed to follow American copyright procedures, putting the book in the public domain immediately upon its original publication. This allowed U.S. publishers to sell the novel at lower prices, since the only up-front costs were printing and distribution, with no royalties going to Stoker or, later, his estate. In the U.K., the book remained under copyright until 1962.

Even after Florence Stoker's efforts, copyright and appropriation troubles with *Dracula* persisted. In an effort to "reestablish creative control," Stoker's great-grandnephew, Canadian Dacre Stoker, co-wrote the 2009 novel *Dracula: The Un-Dead* with screenwriter Ian Holt. The novel, a sequel to *Dracula* set 25 years after the Count's death, is composed of "Bram Stoker's own handwritten notes for characters and plot threads excised from the original edition" supplemented by their own research. This was a huge departure for Dacre Stoker. Before his "writing debut," he had been a Pentathlon world champion and later a track and field coach for the Canadian Pentathlon team.

-------------------------------

Though Dracula is the first notable and, unquestionably, the most popular vampire of all time, Bram Stoker was in fact rather late to the vampire literary milieu[150].

Starting in the late 17th century and building steam throughout the 18th century, vampirism, then considered a genuine infection/condition by the way, was a hot topic in Eastern Europe, particularly in Hungary and the Balkans, where reports were reaching epidemic proportions. Travelers returning from these areas accelerated the spread of vampire gossip to Germany, Italy, France, Spain, and eventually England. Being that fear, superstition and/or fascination with vampires persists to this day, one can only imagine the hysteria it created back in a simpler time. More on that later.

Since life and people's analytical skills were less... let's say "pragmatic" back then, officials and doctors had no choice but to take the vampire outbreak seriously and began to openly study the phenomenon. Meanwhile, sensing a

---

[150] This is a situation I can empathize with. If I had any brains, I'd have written this book five years ago, before "Twilight" and "True Blood" both whimpered to disappointing endings.

treasure trove (and potential riches) in this new, possibly authentic horror material, authors and playwrights started incorporating vampire themes into their work.

Eighteenth-century German poets were among the first to milk the "vampire craze" for material, including *The Vampire* (1748) by Heinrich August Ossenfelder, *Lenore* (1773) by Gottfried August Bürger, and *Die Braut von Corinth* (The Bride of Corinth; 1797) by Johann Wolfgang von Goethe. The first involves a douche-y guy threatening a pious maiden with vampirism to get her to reject her mother's Christian teachings and run off with him for, presumably, sexual experimentation, and the latter two follow a theme of an un-dead spouse or admirer returning to bite, suck and transform their former loves into vampire companions.

Long-form precursors and likely influences on Stoker's novel included John Polidori's *The Vampyre* (1819), which first used the aristocrat-turned-vampire theme; James Malcolm Rymer's *Varney the Vampire* (1847), a massive, serialized Gothic horror book composed of story pamphlets (a.k.a. "penny dreadfuls") published in 1845-47; and Sheridan Le Fanu's *Carmilla* (1871), about a lesbian vampire who preys on a lonely young woman[151]. So, while Stoker's novel eventually went multi-platinum, or whatever happened to popular books in those days, he had the luxury

---

[151] They turn every other damn thing into a movie, why not this captivating tale? Preferably starring Rosario Dawson and Emily Blunt? (Which character each one plays isn't important.)

of absorbing and building on more than a century of vampire material from previous writers.

Part of Stoker's brilliance was staging the origin of Dracula in enigmatic Transylvania, meaning "The Land Beyond the Forest," a region the West generally viewed as a distant, backwater, hillbilly corner of Europe at the time. In fact, the area was still more or less living in medieval conditions when Stoker was amassing research for his novel. The Ottoman Empire had only recently been ejected from the Balkans after Russia crushed them in the Russo-Turkish War. Local people still held onto what they believed to be legitimate superstitions dating back to the Dark Ages, including a rich canon of vampire lore such as the seventh-born child being particularly susceptible to vampirism, identifiable by a hoof as a foot or a tail. It's a shame Stoker never traveled to the Balkans, as he would have had found an incredible wealth of material to absorb and repurpose for his novel.

On the subject of lost research opportunities, it was long believed that Stoker borrowed many traits for his antagonist from our friend Prince Vlad Ţepeş Dracula, however it's now argued that Stoker may have had little more than passing knowledge of the Prince. In *Who Was Dracula?: Bram Stoker's Trail of Blood* (2013), Jim Steinmeyer postulates that Stoker likely first encountered the name "Dracula" in a volume entitled *An Account of the Principalities of Wallachia and Moldavia* (1820) by William Wilkinson, a former British counsel to Bucharest. This book is also likely where Stoker discovered the (mis)information that "Dracul" meant devil, instead of dragon.

According to Stoker's abundant notes, before he found Wilkinson's book, he was planning on calling his book *The Un-Dead* and the antagonist vampire "Count Wampyr." Even after happening upon the almost too-perfect-to-be-true name of Dracula, Stoker's notes seem to indicate he only had scant knowledge of Vlad, rather than having studied the Prince at great length, as many experts formerly believed.

Supporting evidence for this theory is detailed in Steinmeyer's book, describing divergent facts about both Draculae, like the Count being a boyar (a group of people who were in fact mainly Vlad's foes or at least a never-ending irritant), and Castle Dracula being placed in Transylvania instead of Vlad's Wallachia. Then there's Van Helsing's lecture about how the Count was "in life a most wonderful man, soldier, statesman and alchemist," when we know damn well that Vlad was endlessly bloodthirsty, an enthusiastic fan of torture, a prolific impaler, a galloping dick—the list of personal defects goes on.

Steinmeyer believes Stoker actually assembled the character of the Count based on several 19th-century celebrities and friends, who were known to be "dangerous and damaged personalities," thus ideal for a narcissistic, diabolical monster.

Elizabeth Miller, a professor with the Department of English at Memorial University of Newfoundland, agrees with Steinmeyer. Miller has also studied the notes Stoker recorded while laying out the novel and forming the character of Dracula, confirming that none of Stoker's references contain specific information about the life and/or atrocities of Vlad Ţepeş Dracula.

Like Steinmeyer, Miller points out that the absence of Vlad Dracula references in Stoker's otherwise meticulous and copious notes is pretty strong evidence that Vlad's part in conceiving the vampire character was minimal. However, Miller concedes that Stoker acquired and at least skimmed Wilkinson's *An Account of the Principalities of Wallachia and Moldavia* from the Whitby Public Library during a vacation there in 1890. The book refers to one "Voivode Dracula" (the name "Vlad" never appears), who crossed the Danube and attacked Turkish troops. And we know that Stoker's eye almost certainly locked onto a footnote, where Wilkinson incorrectly claims that "Dracul" means "devil" in the Wallachian dialect.

Beyond these items, Professor Miller argues that Stoker doesn't appear to have had any other (documented) exposure to the 15th-century Prince. While one can never know if Stoker got glimpses of Vlad lore from other sources, Miller maintains that he certainly didn't spend extraordinary time researching the Prince for the novel, as was previously believed.

That being said, there is nonetheless compelling evidence, obvious to even a casual reader, suggesting the Draculae are at least somewhat connected. For starters, they share the *same name*. It's known that Stoker spent time at both the Library at Whitby and the British Museum while mining information prior to writing his novel; it would have been difficult not to run across the name Vlad Țepeș Dracula while researching Balkan history, even if he never jotted down the information.

Furthermore, there are the two verified meetings between Stoker and the aforementioned Ármin Vámbéry while he was assembling his novel. It would be difficult to imagine that Vámbéry, maybe after a few cocktails, wouldn't have launched into a few sensationalistic Vlad Țepeș stories during their meetings[152]. However, once again citing Stoker's prolific notes, Miller doubts this occurred.

Parts of the novel appear to display a clear awareness of Țepeș, namely his stories of battling the Turks and the physical resemblances between Count Dracula and depictions of Vlad's appearance (e.g. the extravagant moustache). Yet, Professor Miller notes that Count Dracula's appearance is actually in line with the classic physical descriptions of Gothic literature bad guys and Stoker could have simply borrowed from that material. Furthermore, it's widely believed that Stoker at least partly based Dracula's physical appearance and physique on his employer, Henry Irving.

---

[152] Though I just made up that part about cocktails, a few stiff drinks could easily explain why Stoker didn't come away with any notes on Dracula from these meetings.

If he did indeed have some knowledge or lost notes on Vlad Ţepeş, Stoker undeniably shuffled some of the Prince/Count backstory. This may have been by accident—or possibly intentional, as fiction writers often need to bend details to fit their preconceived story arcs. Again, Miller doubts this, pointing out that Stoker went to great pains to provide thorough and historically accurate detail about England, current events, locations and other details in his novel, presumably to heighten the realism. Stoker's efforts were so meticulous he even studied train schedules, so the details of the team chasing Dracula across the continent back to Transylvania would be consistent with reality. Had Stoker known about the atrocities of Vlad Ţepeş, Miller argues, surely he would have included that historically accurate information in his novel as well.

If your curiosity about the wretched details of Bram Stoker's life story and the novel's origin hasn't been exhausted by now, I recommend acquiring Jim Steinmeyer's *Who Was Dracula?* which, I sincerely assure you, will definitely exhaust it.

# A Romanian Plays a Romanian

We can't have a lengthy examination of the Count Dracula character without touching on the most famous actor to portray him on stage and screen, Bela Lugosi.

Béla Ferenc Dezső Blaskó (October 20, 1882 – August 16, 1956) was a Hungarian-American, born in Lugoj in today's western Romania. He later mercifully shortened his name to Bela Lugosi, as a tribute to his birth-town. Though the region was actually known as the Kingdom of Hungary, Austria-Hungary at the time of Lugosi's birth, the post-WWI redrawing of borders put Lugosi's hometown squarely in Romania, a conveniently uncanny association with the Transylvanian character he was later most famous for playing.

Lugosi started his acting career playing small stage roles in Hungary and even broke into film in 1917's love story *Leoni Leo*. He fled the country after the failed Hungarian Revolution, rebooting his film career in Weimar Germany. He later boarded a merchant ship, working as a seaman, bound for America.

In America, Lugosi appeared in a few Broadway plays and silent films before he first played the role of Dracula in 1927 in a Broadway adaptation of Bram Stoker's novel. Hollywood studios were in a frenzy to produce and release their new "talkies" at the time, and Lugosi was recruited to appear in Universal Pictures' *Dracula*, released in 1931. The film had a running time of 85 minutes, an ambitious length at the time for a straight-up supernatural horror film without some kind of comic relief or resolution that softened or entirely discredited the supernatural elements.

The film was a hit, which naturally inspired Universal to go on a supernatural-themed, thriller film-making rampage that resulted in *The Mummy* (1932), *The Invisible Man* (1933), *Bride of Frankenstein* (1935), and *The Wolf Man* (1941). Universal concocted rumors that audience members were fainting while watching "Dracula," inspiring even more people to see the film out of morbid curiosity. In truth, the film was notably terrifying for 1931 audiences who had never seen a pure horror film before, made all the more disturbing by Lugosi's thrilling performance.

Like now, the instinct to beat a successful theme to death was irresistible in the 1930s and 40s. Two sequels were eventually made: *Dracula's Daughter* (1936) and *Son of Dracula* (1943), neither of which featured Lugosi. The Count was revived for three more films: *House of Frankenstein* (1944), *House of Dracula* (1945), and *Abbott and Costello Meet Frankenstein* (1948), only the latter of which featured Lugosi, looking quite a bit older, being that 17 taxing years had passed since the original *Dracula*. Though Lugosi played Dracula on screen only twice, he's mistaken for having done so much more often because he played non-Dracula vampires in three other movies during his career[153].

Needless to say, *Dracula's* crazy success shot Lugosi's career into the stratosphere. Unfortunately, his association with Dracula and his lingering Hungarian accent almost immediately typecast him in horror films, usually playing the scowling bad guy, and often set in Eastern Europe. Eventually, the consternated Lugosi was getting only minor roles, mainly so the studio could bank on his name by emblazoning it on the poster ads.

Lugosi was repeatedly teamed up to do films with Boris Karloff, who'd also found mega-stardom by playing a monster in 1931's *Frankenstein*. Lugosi usually played second fiddle, or even fifth fiddle, to Karloff's indomitable fame. Among the few films co-starring Karloff where Lugosi landed major roles were *The Black Cat* (1934), *Son of Frankenstein* (1939), and *The Raven* (1935), where Karloff *still* got top billing even though Lugosi played the lead.

A change in management at Universal and their subsequent dropping of the horror genre combined to put Lugosi's career in further decline. Without his bread-and-butter horror films, Lugosi was demoted to the studio's B-film unit, playing smaller and smaller roles, usually only cast so the film could ride on the tails of his name. Lugosi managed to stay afloat with these roles and some stage work, but his heyday was over. Even these paltry roles stopped coming in as word got around that Lugosi had

---

[153] "Mark of the Vampire" (1935), "The Return of the Vampire" (1944), and "Old Mother Riley Meets the Vampire" (1952).

become addicted to morphine while treating his chronic sciatica.

One last career spike arrived in the form of Ed Wood, who tracked down the all but forgotten and destitute Lugosi in the mid-1950s to star in his films. Around this time, Lugosi decided to enter drug rehab.[154]

Lugosi appeared in three of Wood's films, including donning the Dracula cape one last time while shooting test footage that ultimately ended up in the "staggeringly inept" *Plan 9 from Outer Space* (1959), often referred to as "the worst film in the history of cinema[155]." Unfortunately, Lugosi died of a heart attack before the film began principal photography and the remainder of his role was played by another actor, who covered the lower half of his face with his cape throughout, as Lugosi often did while playing Dracula. Lugosi was buried wearing a Dracula cape, a decision made by his son and fifth(!) wife. He had appeared in a total of 103 films throughout his career.

Tim Burton's comedy-drama biopic *Ed Wood* (1994) brought Lugosi's name back into pop culture one last time. Lugosi was played by Martin Landau, who earned an Academy Award for Best Supporting Actor for the role. According to people close to Lugosi, this depiction of him

---

[154] Fun fact: Lugosi's rehab was partly paid for by Frank Sinatra, even though the two had never met.
[155] Though it's found a small, charitable fan base in the so-bad-it's-good genre.

was inaccurate—namely, Lugosi never cursed, never owned small dogs, and did not sleep in a coffin.

# The Borgo Pass and Bistriţa

I'm sorry to report that the Borgo Pass (a.k.a. Tihuta Pass, aka *Pasul Tihuţa*), located in the Birgau Valley on the border of northeast Transylvania and northwest Moldavia, doesn't at all resemble Stoker's dark, foreboding, sphincter-constricting description in the novel. Quite the opposite, in fact. It's a magnificent drive as well as a popular hiking spot, peaking at 3,840 feet and surrounded by a bucolic festival of rolling green landscapes, tiny traditional villages, aging farmhouses, phallic haystacks, orchards, and wooded mountainsides. This is the kind of place where the word "unspoiled" gets lavishly overused by travel writers trying to encapsulate it, for lack of more suitable adjectives. So, bring your good camera—and a necklace of security garlic if you're the jumpy type.

Driving west into Transylvania from Vatra Dornei in Moldavia—a fashionable spa resort during Habsburg times, now a reemerging holiday destination designed around spas and ski vacations—at the high point of the Pass and pretty much the exact geographic location where Stoker describes Castle Dracula in the novel, sits Hotel Castel Dracula (sic). Arguably Romania's most conspicuous homage to the novel, the hotel was built in the early 1980s by a shrewd entrepreneur, shamelessly catering to people looking for a bit of Dracula shtick during their Romania tour.

For 20-odd years, they changed nothing at Hotel Castel Dracula. As recently as 2008, the small, creaky rooms remained untouched by updates, renovations, or even basic technological advances. Curtains and bedding were flush in hues of cranberry and blood, dark green dragon insignias graced the headboards, and wood furniture that was yard sale-worthy even in the early '80s remained. The slap-dash bathrooms, with "Dracula" embroidered towels, had been neither unslapped nor undashed, and though I didn't test them, the '70s-era standard-issue Soviet Bloc rotary telephones still appeared to be in working order. It was pure, glorious tackiness and I loved it.

Alas, when last I visited, Hotel Castel Dracula had made a rather disappointing concession to the business conference and group tour industry, resulting in a large portion of the hotel's rooms being transformed into homogenous, two- and three-star, characterless boxes reminiscent of, say, a down-market hotel near an Omaha truck stop. Fortunately, they seem to have run out of funds before completing the renovation, though I like to think some clearheaded person with a sense of nostalgia stepped in, and a handful of the original rooms have been preserved. Your back will probably protest the mattress conditions, but I highly encourage spending the night in one of these shabby beauties.

The hotel also has a "crypt" (basement) that has been decked out as a vampire lair, complete with a coffin/bed. People should not partake in the tour if they have serious heart conditions that might be over-stressed by the "surprise" at the end of the tour. An apparently frail Canadian tourist literally died of fright during the tour in the mid-90s.

Other diversions, according to the hotel's website, include the dubiously stimulating "exploring every nook and cranny of the Castel," the even more dubious souvenir browsing in the lobby shop, visiting the outdoor marketplace, the genuinely outstanding hiking and horse riding, diving deep into local handicrafts and folklore, and/or wandering around the local cemetery, presumably at night.

Though Hotel Castel Dracula hosts special events all year, the high point is of course their Halloween gala costume ball. Enthusiasts of the macabre descend on the hotel on October 31st and spend the afternoon getting into their wigs, tuxedo capes, bloody wedding dresses, contusion makeup and what have you, then gather for a reception, which includes vamping group photos, drinks, appetizers, live gypsy music, and a bonfire out in the courtyard. Then the real action starts with an "actual" vampire wedding, conducted by an alleged local monk and a gaggle of chanting nuns.

Afterward, the party kicks off in earnest with more music, dancing, and "surprise Halloween treats." A costume contest is held at midnight for those still standing, after which the party most likely rages on till sunrise—at which time one assumes the vampires, zombies, monsters and still-awake drunks alike all perish, melt, burst into flames, or simply collapse in theatrical fashion.

------------------------------------

The *Dracula*-themed nostalgia tour continues nearly an hour to the west of the Pass along a historic trade route (now a winding, two-lane road), past exquisite eye candy like Lake Colibita, to the town of Bistriţa. The town dates from the 12th century (archeological findings indicate the area has been inhabited since the Neolithic period), but it didn't really get going till the King of Hungary's Saxon colonists started arriving here in 1206, who quickly developed the settlement into a flourishing trading post. Like Sighişoara, Bistriţa soon became one of Transylvania's most important Saxon citadels, complete with daunting walls, defensive towers, and frequent witch trials and executions. If you're asking yourself if witch trials were the medieval, German Saxon equivalent to cocktails and a show, the answer is apparently *"ja."*

Today Bistriţa seems to be a city gripped in a town identity crisis, currently home to about 70,000 souls (as of a 2012 census), but still coasting along like it's just 7,000. One assumes it was closer to the latter size in the late 19th century when Stoker chose this tiny dot on the map to be the disembarkation point for protagonist Jonathan Harker as he makes his way to a ghastly stay at Castle Dracula near the beginning of *Dracula* [156]. The continuity-fixated Stoker no

---

[156] A TripAdvisor one-star rating-worthy work trip if there ever were one.

doubt selected obscure Bistrița after meticulously researching the area for a geographically convenient town that was also connected to the Vienna-Budapest train line.

Before boarding a horse-drawn carriage for the final leg of his path to confinement, torment and functioning as a living, breathing, blood-filled Big Gulp, Harker spends the night in Bistrița at the Golden Crown Hotel (*Hotelul Coroana de Aur*). The Crown was fictional at the time of Stoker's writing, but once again someone has built a hotel using the same name (two-to-one it was the same dude who built Hotel Castel Dracula), so as to squeeze a bit more cash out of *Dracula* super fans dutifully reenacting a journey that Stoker himself never took. You can't miss the Golden Crown, with its balcony-lined, daringly purple façade and unusual size for tourism-starved Bistrița[157]. An additional swoon for Dracula enthusiasts is available in the adjacent restaurant where it's possible to order a "robber steak," Harker's last meal before becoming a meal of sorts himself.

-------------------------------------------------------

In five research trips through Romania for Lonely Planet, I was tasked with visiting Bistrița only once. It's a pleasant place without being particularly interesting, which is probably why it only merits the rare LP research visit. Considering its population, it's less hectic than one would expect and the streets in the center of town are definitely a holdover from simpler days, traffic-wise. If you're driving

---

[157] One hundred and ten rooms!

your own vehicle, as you likely will if you've found your way here (keep reading), be prepared to be locked in perpetual confusion and mild alarm while trying to decipher street signs, lights and right-of-way at confounding intersections seemingly plotted out back when local traffic was composed of seven cars and 1,927 horse-drawn carts.

While it *is* technically possible to get to Bistrița by train, it takes a rather impressive amount of dedication. The city sits on a near-forgotten train line that connects nothing important to soporific obscurity. Getting there from high-profile places like Cluj-Napoca or Bucharest requires seven to 10 hours and two or more transfers. As such, the few tourists who see the city usually blow through in a rental car while on a particularly indulgent, off-the-beaten-path road trip or are just bookending their pilgrimage to Hotel Castel Dracula. Fewer still stay the night. As a result, the vibe in Bistrița is generally super chill and, as of my last visit, still disappointingly stuck in what Romania travel old-timers will recognize as the classic pseudo-adversarial approach to hospitality when customer service was reluctant at best and hostile at worst.

In terms of extra-Dracula tourist activities, Bistrița is a quick visit. My one research visit took me barely four hours to complete, and that included a lazy lunch[158].

Once you've Instagrammed and selfied the living crap out of the Golden Crown, head for the old town to get a load

---

[158] Yes, I got the robber steak. It was just OK.

of the surviving 15th- and 16th-century merchants' houses and what remains of the 13th-century fortress walls. The County Museum is one of the most pitiable in Romania. Save yourself that ticket money and get a drink on Piaţa Centrala instead.

It's no Braşov or Sibiu, but Piaţa Centrala, the core of Bistriţa's old town, is quite photogenic. The square's north side is lined with thirteen lovely 15th and 16th-century squat, portico-ed buildings, which once served as trade shops and now house eating and drinking establishments, shops and galleries.

If you're not already churched out, the impressive, Saxon-built Gothic evangelical church (*Biserica Evanghelica*), leisurely built over 100 years in the 15th- and 16th centuries, is also worth an appreciative pause. It's usually locked up outside of worship hours, but the exterior is quite attractive since its recently completed facelift. Its slow-motion, funds-starved renovation suffered a considerable setback in 2008 when the 250-foot (76.5 meter) stone bell and clock tower[159] caught fire. The tower wouldn't have normally lit up so extravagantly, it being made of stone and all, if not for the accelerant provided by the wooden scaffolding surrounding it at the time[160]. Seeing the tower today, however, all scrubbed down and freshly plastered, you'd never know it was recently a giant Roman

---

[159] The tallest in Romania.
[160] Seriously, Google it. It was quite the sight.

candle. If you manage to get inside, you can absorb the collection of 23 flags belonging to the town's former craft guilds, Renaissance-style pews dating from 1516, and the 500-year-old organ.

A few blocks to the northeast is Piaţa Unirii, which is home to the ancient (circa 1280), uncharacteristically humdrum Orthodox Church. If it's open, take a gander at the stone carvings in the chancel and the apse, done in the Cistercian (early Gothic) style. The restored interior is otherwise in the baroque style, with some preserved murals from the late 14th century.

The surviving remains of Bistriţa's 13th-century city walls can be found on the north and west edges of the sweeping park on the city's south side. The walls and the 18 towers were in bad shape after repeated attacks by Turks and Tartars in the 16th and 17th centuries. Then the Austrians arrived in the early 17th century in some kind of grumpy mood and really went to town, smashing large portions to bits. Still in a pissy, demolishing mood in the mid-19th century, the Imperial Court of Vienna ordered the citadel's miraculously still-standing gates to be torn down[161].

Of the 18 defensive towers, only Coopers' Tower (*Turnul Dogarilor*) still stands today, located in the southern half of the park[162]. Built lackadaisically from 1465

---

[161] Man, Austrians can hold a grudge, can't they?
[162] Hint: don't go scanning the sky from a distance to find this thing. A "tower" was about three or four stories high in the 15th century.

to 1575, Cooper's Tower now curiously houses a collection of folklore masks and puppets (*Galeria de Masti si Papusi*).

Once you've respectfully admired every notable blade of grass in Bistriţa, though I'm sure some would disagree, your next best objective is Cluj-Napoca, a buzzing university town with a particular penchant for cafes, nightclubs and art as well as some of the country's best hostels, if that's your thing.

# Epilogue – The Draculae Legacy in Romania

Count Dracula's legacy in Romania is spotty, complicated, and not always welcome by its citizens. With Count Dracula-related connections to the country being wholly invented, Romanians tend to get a little irritated that this is one of the primary associations foreigners make with their country. It's roughly the equivalent of everyone's first, and sometimes only, association with England being the Spice Girls. Romania was so incensed by Count Dracula's rising fame infringing on their treasured culture and history that the *Dracula* novel was not translated into Romanian nor sold in any form inside the country until after the fall of its communist leadership in 1989.

In truth, outside of south-central Transylvania, northern Wallachia, and maybe Bucharest International Airport, you'd be hard pressed to find someone selling a Dracula coffee mug or ashtray, even in gift shops.

That said, the Romanian National Tourist Office has little choice but to work with what they've got. While their incredible mountains, hiking, skiing, culture, and historic fortified churches remain all but anonymous to the outside world, they frequently end up leaning on the Dracula crutch. The most notorious of these endeavors was the aforementioned "Dracula Land" theme park.

With vampire shtick having peaked in pop culture once again, however, Romania's tourism board has begun kicking around new Dracula schemes, claiming public perception has changed. The familiar chorus of how Dracula attractions, particularly in Transylvania, could be the nation's biggest tourism-sector enticement and revenue earner is also being thrown around.

A 2013 press release from the Romanian Federation of Tourism and Service Employers (FPTS) detailed how authorities in six Transylvanian counties were pushing for a project simply called "Dracula," to run from 2014-2020, which they hoped to pay for with unspecified European Union funding.

Here's one of the more unwaveringly definitive excerpts from the FPTS press release:

"The Dracula brand existed for a long time, we only need to exploit it and wrap it properly and then sell it in a modern manner. The highest problem so far in doing this was the hesitation of a certain part of the public opinion in associating Romania with the legend surrounding Vlad Tepes. However, this perception finally changed, so that it is now time we take advantage of a famous myth worldwide and use it to our own benefit. The Dracula project to promote Transylvania as tourism destination represents the most profitable development strategy that can be found for the tourism in this region and we must manage it properly, without hesitations or preconceptions."

See what I mean? They might as well have said "Shut up! No debate, just let us have our Dracula stuff! [cape flourish]" As of spring 2016, no major Dracula tourism initiative had been launched or even teased.

It's understandable that Romanians might cringe at the thought of demeaning one of their greatest national heroes by associating him with a cape-wearing velvet enthusiast. That said, shameless tourism profiteering off legends, fake creatures, and doubtful events has a long, glorious history in tourism going back to, oh, Jesus for starters. I have no doubt that "tour guides" descended on Jerusalem in droves in the 1st century AD to hassle visitors, aggressively offer tours of the big Jesus sites, lead them to the gift shop owned by their brother, and then finally cajole then into dinner at their uncle's restaurant.

Even today, people travel insane distances and spend stupid amounts of money to *not* witness imaginary supernatural attractions. Bigfoot tourism is mushrooming as I write this, including week-long "hunts." Point Pleasant, West Virginia actually erected a public art piece of the Mothman. UFO tourism is still booming in Roswell, New Mexico.

And then there's the mother of them all, the Loch Ness Monster, a tourism cash cow so huge that local tourism competition has become cutthroat, vying for the spoils from the roughly *one million* annual dipshit visitors who spend nearly $38 million in the region for the opportunity to stare blankly at a lake. Tour operators have gone after each other for faking pictures of the Monster. Naming rights for tourist shops have required legal intervention to be resolved. In 2013 two members of the local Chamber of Commerce had to resign after a cruise-tour owner slammed the Chamber's website for containing too much "science" suggesting that Nessie was a myth.

So, while they might hate themselves a little bit, Romanians wouldn't be the first people to hook tourists with wholly invented attractions. And in their case, they would have their mountains, trekking, skiing, fortified churches, peasant village agro-tourism and, oh yeah, *real* Vlad Dracula sites to fall back on to keep visitors occupied once they've depleted their vampire interest quotient.

------------------------------------

Vampirism long predates the superstitious heyday it enjoyed in the Balkans. Descriptions of reanimated corpses go back for millennia, related by many peoples including the Mesopotamians, Hebrews, Ancient Greeks, and Romans. The condition was blamed on a number of factors, such as suicide, witches, spirits, demons, other evil entities and, of course, being bitten by an existing victim.

In Greece vampires were known as "vrykolakas," in Romania "strigoi." In Balkan folklore, a "dhampir" (a.k.a. dhampyre, dhamphir, or dhampyr) is the progeny that results from a vampire and a human coupling. The word comes from the Albanian language, meaning "to drink with teeth." These creatures have supernatural powers similar to vampires, but without the usual weaknesses. Recent vampire fiction has altered the dhampir concept slightly, depicting them as half-breeds, not full-on vampires.

According to the Oxford English Dictionary, the word vampire (appearing as "vampyre") first appeared in 1734 when it was cited in a travelogue titled *Travels of Three English Gentlemen*. However, the word actually appeared two years earlier in the London Journal on March 11, 1732, in an account of the famous Serbian vampire cases of Arnold Paole and Petar Blagojevich, which I'll get to later. These stories spread from the Balkans into Hungary, Austria, France, and Germany where fictional stories began popping up in poetry and literature.

Descriptions of corpses that people thought to be vampires varied by region. One of the most common attributes included bloating of the body, with dark/purplish skin color. People believed this appearance was due to the vampire's being saturated with blood after a recent feeding. Corpses, presumably having consumed more blood than they could hold, would sometimes even have blood dribbling from the mouth and nose. Also, their hair and nails would continue to grow after death and their teeth would appear to protrude, though they would not become spontaneously sharp, so the concept of fangs wasn't part of the condition. In other cases, a sign of vampirism in a corpse was the lack of decomposition, even after significant time had passed, again combined with plumpness and fresh blood on the face.

When vampires were thought to be present, people engaged in some rather bizarre and complex rituals to detect the vampire before killing them. One documented method involved putting a virgin boy on a virgin stallion, dousing them in extra virgin olive oil, then leading them through a graveyard[163]. When the stallion threw a fit, it signaled that a vampire was buried beneath. A simpler method was searching the ground of a graveyard for telltale holes the vampire used to access their coffin.

Signs that a vampire was loitering in your village could include the suspicious death of cattle, sheep, relatives or neighbors. Occasionally vampire myths would stray into ghost-story material, like invisible entities moving or throwing objects and physically interfering with people while they sleep.

Some Balkan legends, mainly in the south, were driven by the ever sexually frustrated nature of vampires, including the belief that male vampires would seek out and have intercourse with their former wives or with women they found attractive when they were alive. One famous case in Serbia involved a woman who became pregnant after her husband's death, which she blamed on her husband's returning in vampire form for a quickie. (Nice save, lady.) In other cases, Serbian men pretended to be vampires in an attempt to bed women. Bulgarian vampires were said to seek out and deflower virgins.

A variety of amusing vampire defensive measures developed over the years, including a branch of wild rose,

---

[163] I may have made part of that up.

hawthorn plant, sprinkling mustard seeds on one's roof, and the ever-popular methods using garlic, a crucifix, a rosary, and holy water.

Furthermore, people could elude vampires by going inside churches or temples, or, oddly, by crossing running water. Though it wasn't a common theme before *Dracula*, mirrors were also sometimes said to repel vampires. Another myth adopted by Stoker was that vampires could not enter a house or structure without being invited by a mortal. Once invited, however, they could enter the structure whenever they pleased. Like Dracula, the vampires of legend could go out in sunlight without being harmed, though they were generally nocturnal.

Once you had found and immobilized a vampire who was bothering you, there were a number of ways to put them out of their misery. Staking was most common throughout the Balkans, up into the Baltic region, and into Russia. Stakes had to be made of wood, ideally ash, oak, or hawthorn, and driven through the heart, though some regions staked their vampires through the mouth (Russia) or stomach (northern Germany and northeastern Serbia). If you *really* wanted to make sure the vampire wouldn't get up again, you'd decapitate them, a practice developed in Slavic areas and Germany.

As for what to do with the head, you had a few options. Depending on local folklore, you might bury the head between the corpse's feet, under its ass or in an entirely different location, which seems like the most sensible option to me.

Like cuisine or dance moves, regional variants of vampire slaying developed over time. Practices might include pouring boiling water over the grave, incinerating the body, shooting a bullet into the corpse through the closed coffin, drowning, sprinkling holy water on the body, giving the corpse a second funeral, or exorcism. Shoving garlic in the vampire's mouth was ubiquitous around the region. In cases when the damn vampire simply refused to die, the body would be dismembered and the pieces burned, or, appallingly, mixed into water, then given to the family of the deceased to drink, which was believed to be an immunization of some sort.

By the early 18th century, reports of vampires had become frequent all over Eastern Europe and East Prussia. The spread of these delirious tales was particularly strange as this was happening concurrently with the Age of Enlightenment, when Dark Ages myths, superstitions, and supernatural folklore were otherwise fading from popular culture or being actively suppressed. Preemptive grave diggings and stakings became a common practice in some regions.

Two vampire cases, the aforementioned Petar Blagojevich and Arnold Paole of Serbia, gained fame in the 1720-30s when physicians and officials arrived from Austria[164]

---

[164] Austria had absorbed Serbia in the 1718 Treaty of Passarowitz.

to investigate the vampire stories that had all of Europe nervously buzzing and hoarding garlic. Being that knowledge of corpse decomposition was still in its infancy— e.g., rates of decomposition can vary greatly depending on climate, temperature and soil composition—and the villagers' steadfast belief in vampires was so compelling, the Austrian teams must have suffered a brainwashing of sorts and reported back to Austria that vampirism was real.

Blagojevich died at 62, an exceptionally ancient age for the time. His son claimed that Blagojevich later reappeared, asking for food. The ingrate son refused and Blagojevich was found dead the following day. (Another legend claims Blagojevich murdered his son.) But the legend of Blagojevich was only beginning. Nine people in the village died in about eight days, usually succumbing to a strange illness within 24 hours, a few seemingly dying of blood loss. Some lived just long enough to claim in their final breaths that Blagojevich had attempted to suffocate them.

Paole was a soldier-turned-farmer who claimed to have survived a vampire attack some years before his death. He reportedly "cured" himself of the vampire affliction by eating soil from the vampire's grave and smearing the vampire's blood on his body. Within weeks of Paole's death, some 16 people in the village died of what they believed to be the work of a vampire and it was concluded the vampire must be Paole. They dug up Paole and discovered that "fresh blood had flowed from his eyes, nose, mouth, and ears; that the shirt, the covering, and the coffin were completely bloody; that the old nails on his hands and feet, along with the skin, had fallen off, and that new ones had grown." The alarmed villagers staked Paole, which allegedly caused his body to groan and bleed even more, then burned him. They also dug up four of Paole's supposed victims and did the same to them, for good measure.

The Blagojevich and Paole cases were meticulously documented, signed off by Austrian government officials and published widely across Europe, sparking general panic. Now that it was officially legitimized, the fears and superstitions of villagers and even ostensibly learned city folk alike went hypersonic, with new reports of vampirism mushrooming. The ensuing clusterfuck hysteria is now known as the "18th-Century Vampire Controversy."

More Austrian officers and doctors arrived to investigate supposed outbreaks. One doctor admirably kept his wits about him for a while, sensibly concluding the people were likely dying of malnutrition, a common problem in the region, combined with the masochistic Eastern Orthodox practice of severe fasting[165]. However, the doctor's resolve broke upon examining corpses that didn't appear to be decomposing, while more recently deceased corpses showed normal decomposition. It was also discovered that some organs were filled with fresh blood instead of

---

[165] Remember how poor, apparently reanimated Blagojevich just wanted a little food? What are the chances some village quack declared him dead when he was just *almost* dead and he later woke up with a hankering for a BLT?

coagulated blood. The familiar plumpness, dark/redish/purple-ish color of the skin and the presence of blood around the mouth were once again theorized to be the result of recent feeding.

Of course, these are all conditions now known to be perfectly normal states of decomposition. In addition to variants like skin color and rates of decay, the skin around hair follicles and nails retracts as it becomes dehydrated, making it appear as if hair and nails have grown. Gums recede, giving the effect of larger teeth. Nails sometimes fall off. Bodies swell as gases created by decomposition build up in the torso and this pressure forces blood to ooze from orifices (e.g., the nose and mouth). In cases when the person was thin or sick late in life, as people usually were in those hungry times, this swelling could have the unsettling effect of making the corpse look healthier than it had been prior to death. Then, unsurprisingly, when you plunge a stake into a blood-bloated corpse, you get a Tarantino-esque blood eruption from several orifices and the escaping gas sounds eerily like groaning.

Furthermore, studies also theorize that rabies may have been the cause of vampire-like symptoms in some instances. Vampirism and rabies have several similarities, including hypersensitivity to garlic and light, bloody frothing at the mouth, sleep disorders that effectively make the victim nocturnal, the urge to bite people and even revved-up horniness. Coincidentally, wolves and bats, whose presence was a telltale sign of vampire activity, can carry rabies.

A quick aside: While three species of so-called vampire bats do exist, they are only found in South America[166], so this particular association would have been pure myth in 18th-century Europe. Meanwhile, the blissfully vampire-free people of South America were probably indifferently roasting these things on sticks over a fire. Or at least using them for target practice.

If you're chuckling to yourself about all those gullible simpletons of the 18th century, hold that thought.

In Bulgaria, over 100 "vampire skeletons" have been exhumed at various sites over time, staked with iron rods. The practice, which started sometime in the Middles Ages, persisted into the first decade of the 20th century and only ceased after the government expressly banned it. It's believed the practice is probably still occasionally, quietly employed in more superstitious corners of the country.

In early 1970 the local press started printing stories that London's Highgate Cemetery was home to vampires. Hastily equipped vampire hunters and gawkers descended on the cemetery to ostensibly deal with the problem—or, possibly, get their picture taken with a sexy vampire. Naturally, profiteering soon followed, including a book written by one Sean Manchester, who was among the first to fan the "Highgate Vampire" rumors and claimed to have once exterminated a whole nest of vampires in the area[167].

---

[166] And they got their name from the Old World folklore vampire bats, incidentally.
[167] Pics or it didn't happen, Sean.

In 2002-03, vampire attacks were reportedly occurring across the West African nation of Malawi. In one case, a crazed mob stoned someone to death and attacked at least four other people suspected of being vampires. Even the Governor was attacked after rumors got around that the government was somehow in cahoots with the vampires.

In January 2005, reports of multiple supposed vampire bites, eventually dismissed as urban legend, briefly gripped Birmingham, England. *The Guardian* wasted no time debunking the "rumours," saying, "Last month, this 'vampire' went on a 'rampage' in Glen Park Road, Ward End. The attacker reportedly bit a male pedestrian and then bit neighbours who came to the man's aid. One woman had 'chunks' bitten out of her hand, according to reports, which feature lots of one-word 'quotes' and very little in the way of named sources."

A local rag, The Birmingham Evening Mail, giddily egged the story on, writing, "As the sun dips below the rooftops of sleepy terraced streets, residents rush home, quickly gathering up playing children, because after night falls a vampire hungry for blood stalks. Reports of a Dracula-style attacker on the loose biting innocent people has spread terror throughout neighbourhoods in Birmingham, causing many to fear the darkness of the night."

Local police quickly announced that no crimes of that description had been reported and hospitals chimed in saying they hadn't treated any such victims. This didn't stop some of the more suggestible citizens from becoming temporarily unwound.

Finally, belief in vampires is widespread in Serbia to this day, with documented reports occurring on a regular basis. One case made it onto ABC News during a presumably slow news day in 2012, when the tiny village of Zorazje in western Serbia went to pieces after a water mill, which was believed to be the home of a notorious vampire named Sava Savanovic, collapsed. The villagers concluded that Savanovic was likely searching for a new home, putting them in danger. "People are very worried," said local municipal assembly member Miodrag Vujetic. "Everybody knows the legend of this vampire and the thought that he is now homeless and looking for somewhere else and possibly other victims is terrifying people. We are all frightened."

Fearful villagers were said to be hanging holy crosses and icons above the entrances to their homes, rubbing their hands with garlic, and arming themselves with hawthorn stakes or thorns.

Say what you will, but given the choice between being surrounded by that sort of weirdness or in the midst of the current paranoia-fueled gun-nut hijinks in the U.S., I'll take the people of Zorazje every time.

The nerds, of course, couldn't resist weighing in. In 2006, physics professor Costas Efthimiou of the University of Central Florida in Orlando, with the help of a grad student, published a paper proving that vampires can't possibly exist. Using geometric progression and the random supposition that the first vampire in the world had been created on January 1, 1600, Efthimiou argued that even if vampires fed only once a month, far less than myth suggests, and every victim was infected, every human on the planet (roughly 537 million at the time) would be transformed into a vampire within two and a half years. Of course, as any halfwit knows, the gaping hole in their theory is that the vampire infection isn't necessarily passed along *every* time a vampire feeds. In your face, math!

How are these absurd stories given even an ounce of value in this day and age? Thanks to the programmable nature of our ape-brains, ceaseless theme/concept/story repetition can often result in a very fine line between reality and myth. I'll spare you my atheist-bent diatribe that I'd normally insert here and instead simply point out that contemporary people are likely so easily convinced of vampire activity due to the non-stop deluge of vampire-themed books, TV shows and films. Here's an exceedingly abridged list of popular vampire entertainment from just the past 70 years:

- Richard Matheson's novel *I Am Legend* (1954), adapted into three movies: *The Last Man on Earth* starring Vincent Price in 1964, *The Omega Man* starring Charlton Heston in 1971, and *I am Legend* starring Will Smith in 2007.
- *The Vampire Chronicles* (1976–2014) novels by Anne Rice, including *Interview with the Vampire* (1976), *The Vampire Lestat* (1985), *The Queen of the*

*Damned* (1988), and *Prince Lestat* (2014), a few of which were adapted into films of varying merit.

- *The Hunger* (1981) a novel by Whitley Strieber, adapted into a film in 1983 starring David Bowie and Susan Sarandon.
- The *Blade* three-movie series (1998-2004).
- The cult film *Buffy the Vampire Slayer* (1992), developed into a cult-ier TV series (1997-2003), both created by Joss Whedon.
- Elizabeth Kostova's wildly popular novel *The Historian* (2005).
- Swedish author John Ajvide Lindqvist's novel *Låt Den Rätte Komma* (2004), adapted into a Swedish film called *Let the Right One In* (2007) and an American film titled *Let Me In* (2010).
- The "Twilight Saga" five-film series (2008-12).

Throw in dozens of lesser-known novels, comic books, Marilyn Manson, and so forth and one can understand how this incessant repetition rewires our brains into (almost) believing such things.

------------------------------

Vlad "The Impaler" Dracula, it should go without saying, remains one of the greatest figures in Romania's history. His appalling deeds notwithstanding, Vlad is widely considered a national hero in Romania to this day, most recently having been honored as one of the "100 Greatest Romanians" in 2006 by the *Mari Români* (Great Romanians) television series[168]. Besides, what's the statute of limitations on grudges for even advanced-level atrocities in the name of defending one's homeland[169]? Two centuries? Three? I think we can safely declare Vlad forgiven of fault in regards to wartime atrocities during a lavishly atrocious era.

After his death, while Dracula was elevated to hero status at home, his legacy once again took a beating in Western Europe and even in Russia, via the previously mentioned entertainment rags. Tales written decades after his death described Vlad as a wild, unrepentant fiend who frequently went on indiscriminate, horrific murdering rampages; destroyed fortresses and churches[170]; and habitually burned villages and whatever else he could conceivably set alight.

A German pamphlet from 1521, the equivalent of an adult comic book of the time, published a rather distant 44 years after Dracula's death, said:

> "He roasted children, whom he fed to their mothers. And (he) cut off the breasts of women, and forced their husbands to eat them. After that, he had them all impaled."

---

[168] Though this same series also elected to honor Nicolae "Wrong Way" Ceauşescu, who, after viewer voting, ranked one spot *ahead* of Vlad on the list! So, clearly the people of Romania aren't necessarily in full agreement as to Dracula's impact on their country. And Nicolae's, come to that. Stephen the Great landed at Number 1, incidentally.

[169] Mostly.

[170] OK, that part is difficult to argue.

Detractors happily spread this gossip as fact, conveniently forgetting that they'd likely be crouching in muddy trenches, crossing swords with Ottomans if not for Vlad's tenacious heroics in the Balkan Peninsula.

Near-fictional stories like this, which were written in a time when accurate reportage of history was sketchy at best, doomed Vlad to centuries of revulsion. In all fairness, Dracula's grand total body count didn't help in preserving his good name.

The number of people Dracula was ultimately responsible for killing varies wildly, starting at 40,000 and going up to and beyond 100,000. It's difficult to fathom how it could be 100,000[171], but from the cumulative incidents described in previous chapters[172], it's likely *way* more than 40,000. Today, in a world of seven billion people, such a death toll would be horrifying yet still a relatively paltry tally to accumulate in just under seven years. But considering population numbers in the 15th century[173], he was a goddamn mushroom cloud-laying slaughterbot. Other massacres in the 15th, 16th and even the 18th centuries can't touch Dracula's astoundingly efficient murder rate. Though he ultimately had a much larger grand total, even 16th

---

[171] That would have meant over 16,000 killings per year of his reign or about 45 murders per day. Even Dracula wasn't that prolific.

[172] Which, rest assured, were diligently fact checked, but who really knows? Honestly, fact checking some parts of this book was like trying to parse the truth from a 600-year-old TMZ report.

[173] Wallachia at the time had maybe 500,000 inhabitants.

century lunatic Ivan the Terrible can't touch Dracula's yearly average[174].

In addition to centuries of relentless trolling by critics and artistic license taken by hack writers, Dracula's questionable reputation endured a renewed pounding when an Irish author saw fit to level-up his already muddy historical characterization into literal monster territory.

-------------------------------

Whatever his shortcomings, the post-Dracula world probably missed him something fierce. All of Dracula's blood-spilling and clever battle savviness ultimately only temporarily held off Ottoman rule of Romania. Not long after mounting Vlad's head on a pike and doing the equivalent of a cartoonish, full-armed brow-wipe, the Turks were soon back on track to stampede over all of Christian Europe. They beat up on Hungary in the 16th century and soon claimed Transylvania. As always, the affected locals were allowed autonomy, assuming they continued to cough up cash tributes to the Sultan. Wallachia and Moldavia were also forced to pay tributes to the Turks in order to keep autonomy, which kept out permanent Turkish occupying forces[175].

---

[174] And Ivan is credited for many killings that he merely ordered from far-off locations, whereas for the most part Dracula gave his victims a more, ahem, personal touch.

[175] As well as virtually any trace of Turkish culture, architecture and so forth in case you're wondering why there aren't ethnic Turkish communities and mosques dotting Romania today.

In 1594, combined forces from Wallachia, Moldavia, and Transylvania led by Mihai Viteazul (Michael the Brave; ruled 1593-1601) successfully overran Turkish strongholds[176]. A truce was called with the Ottomans in 1595, and an internal power struggle among the three principalities ensued almost immediately, opening the door for a joint Habsburg-Transylvanian noble army to waltz in and take over Transylvania. But the Turks mounted a strong and lasting comeback, sweeping across Romania and Hungary before they were defeated at the gates of Vienna in 1687. The resulting massive change in power landed Transylvania firmly under Habsburg rule.

The 18th century was filled with serf revolts, marking the start of Transylvanian Romanians' fight for political emancipation[177]. Meanwhile Ottoman-protected Wallachia was enjoying relative peace and prosperity punctuated by a cultural and artistic renaissance that started under the reign of Constantin Brâncoveanu (ruled 1688-1714). Up north, poor Moldavia was being diced up, losing its northern territory (Bucovina) to Austria-Hungary and its eastern territory (present-day Republic of Moldova) to Russia.

The Russians and Turks stopped trash-talking and finally went head-to-head in 1828-29, and for a time Wallachia and Moldavia were Russian protectorates while

---

[176] On the tail of this brotherly cooperation, the three principalities were briefly united in 1600.

[177] Habsburg Emperor Joseph II finally abolished serfdom in Transylvania on August 22, 1785.

remaining in the Ottoman Empire, a discombobulating state which must have been a hoot for the inhabitants.

Transylvania got caught up in the Hungarian revolution in 1848, as Hungary tried to end Habsburg domination. Feeling revolution fever, Romanians started their own campaign for political emancipation and equality. The Habsburgs convinced Transylvania's Romanians to go after the Hungarian revolutionaries in Transylvania, with the incentive of national recognition in return. Transylvanian Romanians agreed, enthusiastically assaulting Transylvanian Hungarians with a mind for some good ol' fashioned vengeance for centuries of ethnic mistreatment. Russia stepped in and ended this arrangement, opening the door for Austria-Hungary to take control of Transylvania, ruling from Budapest. The Hungarian language was imposed on the Romanians and anyone who resisted was punished[178].

Outside that hotspot, Wallachia and Moldavia quietly prospered, albeit while sending regular boatloads of cash to appease the Sultan. In 1859, Alexandru Ioan Cuza was elected to lead both Moldavia and Wallachia, creating on December 11th, 1861 a noncontiguous, but united, national state known as the United Romanian Principalities. They wisely shortened the name to Romania in 1862. Cuza was

---

[178] Imagine for a minute that your national language changes overnight and using your native language suddenly becomes punishable. Yeah, huge dick move.

ousted four years later and Prussian Prince Carol I stepped
in.

Having had just about enough of their landlord,
Romania joined Russia in the Russo-Turkish War (1877-78)
and finally freed themselves of Ottoman rule. The victory
swoon continued as the country extended its borders to the
Black Sea by acquiring parts of Dobrogea in a trade with
Russia in return for Bessarabia (now the Republic of
Moldova) a year later.

Romanian independence was recognized under the
Treaty of San Stefano at the Congress of Berlin in 1878. In
1881 it was declared a kingdom. Carol I was promoted and
declared the first king of Romania.

Still on a roll, Romania swelled further when it
absorbed yet more of the Black Sea region of Dobrogea, after
lending a hand in the brief Second Balkan War against
Bulgaria in 1913. Apart from that skirmish, the late 19th and
early 20th centuries were an amazingly calm and
industrious time in the region. One assumes, however,
Romania kept vigilant watch on its powerful neighbors
Austria-Hungary, Russia and the Ottomans, any one of
which could have marched in and taken control of massive
parts of the country in, like, a week.

Romania's cascade of misplaced, conflicting alliances
in both WWI and WWII were, in short, disastrous. The
whiplashing details of these decades could on their own fill a
book. Suffice it to say, despite miraculously acquiring more

land when the dust of the wars settled, Romania suffered incredible military losses.

Greatly weakened, and beholden to Russia for saving its wartime bacon, Romania fell under communist rule and began a shameful era of legendary corruption and nationalist fervor that included the rise of the brutal, anti-Semitic Iron Guard.

With Moscow effectively at the wheel, Romania's Communist Party swelled from just one thousand members to over one million bandwagoneers in 1945. This newly powerful political force wasted little time in forcing then-King Michael to abdicate under extreme duress, ejecting him from the country and rebranding themselves as the Romanian People's Republic.

After furiously capturing and locking up all pre-war leaders, prominent intellectuals and suspected dissidents[179], the communists embarked on their whimsical, ill-considered, violent, often incompetent reign. While the country thrashed and flailed trying to figure out communism, the old-hand Soviets hung out in the wings, hauling away all the Romanian resources they could get their hands on under the veil of the "SovRom" agreements, which established "joint" Soviet-Romanian companies that made the looting appear business-related.

After reluctantly putting the drill down and reading the manual, Romania managed to assemble a stable

---

[179] Or working them to death.

government. Using what was no doubt judicious persuasion, Romanian leader Gheorghe Gheorghiu-Dej convinced the USSR's Nikita Khrushchev to withdraw Soviet troops from the country in 1958.

About the same time, the rapid political rise of Nicolae Ceaușescu began, leading him to securing the role of Secretary General of Romania's Communist Party in 1965 and finally President on December 9, 1967.

After a brief honeymoon period, Ceaușescu's reign took a turn of cruelty, becoming one of the most tyrannical in the ex-Soviet bloc. Dissent was emphatically squashed largely due to the actions of the Securitate, which grew to be one of the most vicious police forces in the world. At the height of its power, the Securitate employed roughly 11,000 agents and had about a half-million active informers. For a country of about 22 million, that's a lot of informers. In short, national paranoia soared[180].

After 25 years of Ceaușescu's brutal, megalomaniac, sometimes comically half-witted antics, the hot Latin blood finally kicked in and the quick, resolute Romanian Revolution commenced in late 1989[181]. It took 15 additional corruption-fueled years for Romania to show signs of recovery and progress, which was rewarded (some say

---

[180] One can only imagine how a reanimated Dracula would have dealt with this social and economic devastation of his country, but it would have presumably involved a lot of entrails tasting fresh air.
[181] Recounted at great length in the Târgoviște chapter.

prematurely) by being granted European Union membership in 2007.

In 2014, after years of false promises about combating the startling ongoing fraud and exploitation of EU funds, Romania's long-promised attack on corruption finally began in earnest. The National Anti-Corruption Directorate (DNA), established in 2002, finally grew some balls in the form of Laura Codruta Kovesi, a former teenage girls' basketball prodigy who became head of the DNA in April 2013. Kovesi oversaw myriad arrests of high-level officials in the face of heavy political pressure to back off and personal attacks in the media. In 2014 alone, the DNA indicted and convicted 1,138 people, logging a rather amazing 90 percent conviction rate, which included a top judge, 24 mayors, five members of parliament, two ex-ministers, a sitting finance minister, and Romania's richest man.

Among the heavy hitters receiving jail time was former underachieving Prime Minister Adrian Nastase, convicted for taking bribes (four years) and blackmail (three years). At the time of his sentencing, Nastase had only just gotten out of prison after serving time for a previous conviction in 2012, which he almost avoided by attempting suicide. His wife was also convicted of collusion, but got away with a three-year suspended sentence.

Even more high-profile was the case against Elena Udrea, former protégée (and, allegedly, ex-girlfriend/mistress/"very close friend") of ex-president

Traian Basescu, who served as Tourism Minister from 2008 to 2009 and as Regional Development and Tourism Minister from 2009 to 2012. At the time of writing, Udrea was being detained on charges of helping to launder millions of dollars with her former husband, acquired by overcharging the government for software. She made headlines again within a week of her arrest when she asked that her cell be painted and wallpapered. In what was probably an exasperated move to get her out of their hair, Udrea was transferred to house arrest while she was investigated.

And the far and away most giddying highlight (so far) occurred in September 2015, when sitting Prime Minister Victor Ponta was indicted on charges of forgery, money laundering, and being an accessory to tax evasion during his time as a lawyer.

The DNA has taken on cult hero status in Romania, particularly among frustrated young people yearning to free themselves from the legacy of corruption and bureaucracy perpetrated by aging officials who won't retire quickly enough. Despite the DNA's incredible progress, Romania came in 69th on the corruption index produced by Transparency International in 2014[182], the same position it held in 2013.

Though the situation is increasingly encouraging, Romania is still trying to find its feet even now. Parts of Romania are developing so rapidly that the guidebook

---

[182] Out of 175 countries.

chapters for some cities need to be completely thrown out and rewritten every three or four years. The scales tipped from a majority rural population to urban in just the past decade, and only just[183].

While construction and breathtaking westernization race forward in cities, the rural and peasant populations are still coping with dizzying new farming and livestock rules brought on by EU membership, not to mention trying to maintain their identity in the face of iPhones, Google and, Red Bull. The juxtaposition of BMWs and horse-drawn carts jockeying for position on city streets (neither one looking out for the other) is fading fast, as the government steadily expands horse-cart bans on the roads so BMW drivers can get to their destinations 25 seconds faster. Hoardes of Paris Hilton and Vin Diesel wannabes lounge in cafes, apparently unburdened by jobs or schooling, with dazed and even openly wistful Ceaușescu-era survivors sitting in clutches on park benches, wondering what the fuck is going on.

But as I've always said, living in Romania isn't the same as visiting Romania. It's arguably the biggest bang for your buck left in Europe. An amazing number of historic churches and ruins somehow survived communist demolition, exploitation whims, and neglect. The beauty of the Carpathian Mountains is comparable to the Alps. The roughly 23 different ecosystems, towns, and villages in the

---

[183] Romania's urban population stood at an estimated 52.8 percent in 2011, according to the CIA World Factbook

Danube Delta (Europe's second largest delta) are a singular time-warp experience. Rural life continues in some communities more or less as it was 100 years ago and before. Every single day of travel in Romania is weird, amazing, sad, fascinating, infuriating, old, new, and just plain fun.

-------------------------------------------

Outside of Romania, contemporary nods to Vlad Dracula are largely folded into works of fiction.

Despite being an adaptation of Bram Stoker's novel, the 1992 Francis Ford Coppola film *Bram Stoker's Dracula* diverges from the book and tacks on a prologue indicating the Prince and Count are in fact the same person. The film opens in Transylvania[184] in 1462 as Vlad is kissing his wife Elisabeta goodbye before racing off to disembowel some Turks. Mirroring the incident at the Poenari siege, while Vlad is off on a staking spree, a conniving Turkish soldier fires a message attached to an arrow through a castle window falsely informing Elisabeta that Vlad is dead. Distraught and fearing enslavement, Elisabeta leaps to her death from the castle into the river valley below.

Vlad returns to find his wife dead and is gravely informed by a priest that, since she committed suicide, Elisabeta's soul cannot enter heaven. Vlad loses his mind, renounces God (who had nothing to do with it), and drives

---

[184] They still didn't bother correcting the Transylvania/Wallachia error, though.

his sword into a stone crucifix, which naturally spews blood all over the floor of the chapel. Vlad, who is now running on some kind of bat-shit crazy instinct, declares he will live for as long as it takes to avenge Elisabeta's death by harnessing the terrible powers of darkness. He gulps down some of the crucifix blood—aaaaannnd fade to black. Then we pick up the novel narrative with Jonathan Harker[185] and it's more or less all Count Dracula from there on out.

Vlad Dracula got a biopic, of sorts, in the 2000 TV movie *Dark Prince: The True Story of Dracula*, filmed in Romania. The film shows restraint, at least at first, portraying Dracula in a sympathetic, tragic light. He gets his taste for blood as the film progresses, but since it's a TV movie they can't go into full-gore exaggeration and show him tearing people's heads off and sucking out their brains through the neck holes. A few cinematic twists aside, the film depicts a relatively accurate outline of his life story. Alas, it wasn't exactly a masterfully acted thrill-ride (the critics hated it), but if you are now a die-hard Vlad fan and absolutely *must* see it, the last time I checked the full movie was available on YouTube.

Elizabeth Kostova's wonderfully suspenseful book, *The Historian*, published in 2005, once again portrays Vlad the Impaler and the vampire Dracula as one. And what a relief it is that someone finally managed to produce something featuring poor Vlad that didn't suck[186].

---

[185] A startlingly baby-faced Keanu Reeves.

In late 2014, soon after I got started on this book, *Dracula Untold* was released in theaters. A fantasy horror film with a generous budget, the film manages to be far more engaging than *The Dark Prince*. Though critics weren't super impressed, the film made a boatload of money anyway. Whatever your film-snobbery quotient, it's a decent 92 minutes of super dark, special effects-driven action, which, assuming plenty of wine, wouldn't be your worst Saturday night ever.

The film starts off with the familiar backstory of Vlad the Impaler pissing off the Turks, who then prepare to obliterate Wallachia. Then it goes *way* off the reservation when Vlad, prepared to do anything to save his people, seeks out an ancient vampire miles up some mountain and is transformed into a mega-supercharged-vampire, capable of obliterating whole armies with the wave of his hand; in the end lots of Turks die horribly.

Outside of film and literature, Vlad Dracula, when he's remembered at all, is difficult to pin down, infamy-wise. Kurt W. Treptow, author of *Vlad III Dracula: The Life and Times of the Historical Dracula* (2000), succinctly describes Vlad as "one of the most controversial figures of fifteenth century Europe[187]. Vlad remains obscured behind a veil of myths, the origins of which can be traced to his own lifetime."

---

[186] Yes, I skipped the pun opportunity there. Too easy.
[187] Which is really saying something.

Dracula managed the remarkable duality of being both champion and villain. And not just to Christian Europe and the Ottomans respectively, because duh, but also to his own people. That his subjects would abandon him while he was still risking his life to drive the Ottomans out of Wallachia must have been accompanied by head-spinning cognitive dissonance.

Though Vlad's reign of less than seven cumulative years may seem disappointingly short, that's still a lot longer than most princes of that era[188]. Still, one can't help feeling perhaps his reign ended too soon. By the same token, if his luck hadn't run out with the Ottomans, you have to wonder how long Vlad would have lasted as a prince without the distractions of war, vengeance and speed-building impenetrable fortresses.

His passion for viciously cleaning house and defending Wallachia was, how shall we say, an excellent diversion for an unchained rage-aholic. Without those tasks to keep him occupied, where would he have channeled that energy? It's difficult to imagine Vlad defeating the Turks, cooling off his berserker rage, settling down, and taking up the harpsichord.

Alternatively, and it pains me to say it[189], it's more likely his hyper-fervor for swift and terrible justice would

---

[188] If you'll recall from way back in chapter three, the average reign for a prince from 1418 until Dracula's second sitting on the throne (1456-1462) was barely over two years.
[189] Because in doing so, I'm likely enraging thousands of proud Romanians.

have been focused squarely on Wallachia, presumably taking a painfully tyrannical direction. If not that, then perhaps getting some guys together and heading up to Transylvania to do a little land-grabbing of his own.

How long would he have lasted on the throne in tyrant/conqueror mode before exhausting the patience of his subjects? Based on Wallachia's previous musical-throne evidence, it seems plausible that before long Vlad would have woken up one morning strapped spread-eagle to his bedposts, surrounded by angry boyars, with a grinning half-brother guiding a lubed stake into his rectum.

Of course, musing about an unattractive alternate legacy had he survived for a prolonged rule still takes nothing away from Dracula's stunning exploits while battling an Ottoman force that, once he was out of the way, rather easily rolled over the Balkans, Wallachia, Transylvania, Hungary and beyond. Think about it: the sheer will of one guy defending a moderately sized region, backed by a mercenary-enhanced ragtag group of farmers, peasants, women, and children, held off a hurricane-caliber force that eventually fought its way to the gates of Vienna. The man was a badass, straight-up force of nature.

Dracula was the right kind of terror at the right time for Wallachia. A supernova of justice[190] at home and a sphincter-collapsing opponent to any invaders who stared longingly at Wallachia for too long. But supernovas aren't

---

[190] Or injustice, depending on which side of the stake you're on.

known for their longevity and even the most affable rulers in
that era weren't opposed to a little brutality and immoral
behavior. One way or another, Dracula's future probably
wasn't going to be rosy. He may have died too soon, but in
doing so he lived just long enough to be a hero to Romania.

# Author Bio

Leif Pettersen is a freelance writer, humorist, insatiable traveler, "slightly caustic" blogger and semi-professional wino from Minneapolis, Minnesota. While reinventing himself as a world-traveling freelance writer, he spent a cumulative two years in Romania, both living in the northeastern city of Iaşi and crisscrossing the country inspecting every notable patch  of grass for inclusion in various Lonely Planet guidebooks. He's visited 55 countries (so far), and has also lived in Spain and Italy.

Pettersen has authored Lonely Planet guidebooks for Tuscany and Moldova, and has been a prolific contributor to LonelyPlanet.com. His work has appeared in *Global Traveler* magazine, MSN, *USA Today*, Mapquest/AOL Travel, CNN Travel, BBC Travel, the *San Francisco Chronicle*, the *Minneapolis Star Tribune*, *Travel + Escape* magazine, the anthology *To Myanmar With Love* (Things Asian Press), *Rough Guide First Time Europe* (6th Edition), *Juggle* magazine, *The Growler* and *vita.mn*.

Pettersen loves chocolate, hates pickles, types with exactly four fingers, and can escape from a straitjacket. In 2014, he won a silver medal at the world juggling championships as one half of the duo Duck and Cover. He has not vomited since 1993, making him a consummate travel journalist and excellent party guest.

# leifpettersen.com

# @leifpettersen

Made in the USA
Lexington, KY
25 August 2016